The State of the State of Illinois, 2006

To Christopher and Kiara

***

The State of the State of Illinois, 2006

Cedric Herring
Editor

Institute of Government and Public Affairs
University of Illinois

2006

Institute of Government and Public Affairs
University of Illinois

Printed in the United States of America.

Contents

Acknowledgments

When I first presented the idea of *The State of the State of Illinois* to colleagues in the Institute of Government and Public Affairs, I was gratified that several thought it was a good idea. Most, however, thought it would be a good idea for 2007 rather than 2006. They thought it was simply impossible to complete in the timeframe I had in mind. But with the capable assistance of Ganga Vijayasiri, Susan Sindelar, Laura Gonzales, Dana Cole, Snow Xu Wang, and Scott Koeneman, publication of *The State of the State of Illinois, 2006* was transformed from a "simply impossible" task into an important *and* timely book. I thank them for their assistance. I also thank Robert Rich, not only for believing that this was an important and doable undertaking, but for his willingness to help underwrite it. Finally, I would like to express my appreciation to the various authors who contributed materials for this book. They all met the unfair deadlines that I imposed. Obviously, without their contributions, this book would not have been possible.

Cedric Herring

Preface

The Institute of Government and Public Affairs (IGPA) at the University of Illinois is committed to research, analysis, and public engagement related to matters of state and local government. Over its fifty-eight year history, IGPA has been deeply involved in examining the most important governmental and policy issues facing Illinois. We have accomplished this through publications, conferences, workshops, and educational seminars. This new volume represents our first attempt at a collection of essays designed to assess trends in critical public policy areas facing Illinois. Each chapter poses some of the following questions: where does Illinois stand in a given policy arena? How does our performance compare with other states and/or the nation as a whole? What are some of the major problems facing Illinois in a given policy area? What are some of the approaches that have been or might be taken to address the issues which have been identified?

The contributions to this volume report on current research undertaken by members of the faculty and staff of IGPA. Our objective is to inform policy deliberations on the key issues facing this state. We welcome the feedback of policy-makers in the public and private sectors, as well as scholars, in the hope of stimulating more discussion of the critical issues in Illinois.

Robert F. Rich
Director
January, 2006

Chapter 1

The State of the State:
Critical Issues Facing Illinois

Cedric Herring

Introduction

There are several issues currently on the Illinois policy agenda confronting decision makers and others who address public issues. In addition, there are many policy choices on the horizon that will require thoughtful analysis and responsible actions on the part of policymakers. What are these issues, and what actions will they require?

The State of the State of Illinois, 2006 provides some answers. It offers insights and analysis of critical issues facing Illinois from the Institute of Government and Public Affairs (IGPA) of the University of Illinois. In this non-technical book, IGPA faculty and associates use their expertise to provide accessible discussions of such pressing issues as the state's economy and structural deficit, especially as they relate to the Illinois state budget and the need to finance state pensions. The book also delves into health policy issues, long-term care, and public financing of mental health and developmental disability services. In addition, IGPA policy experts tackle such issues as child care and after-school services for children and families. This volume also calls attention to the state's conservation policies, as it examines the effectiveness of land retirement policy as an instrument for reducing environmental damages from agricultural production. It also deals with the thorny issue of political corruption and ethics policy in the state. And finally, it provides analyses of emerging issues such as the digital divide by examining the gender gap in information technology as well as the relationship of race to the digital divide and workforce readiness in Illinois.

This first chapter serves two central purposes. First, it provides a summary of some of the major demographic changes that have occurred in the state over the last decade, and it presents an overview of public opinion on several issues on the public agenda in Illinois as measured by results from the Illinois Policy Survey. In doing so, it shows how various groups in Illinois view policy issues and what they believe should be done about them.

The second assignment of this opening chapter is to fulfill the more traditional task of providing a preview of the contributions that comprise this volume. In that section of this chapter, I provide a synopsis of the wide range of policy issues discussed in the remaining chapters of this book.

Demographic Changes and Policy Preferences in Illinois

Illinois is a geographically dispersed and demographically diverse state. Not everyone will agree on what the critical issues confronting the state are, nor will there be consensus on what the policy solutions are to these issues. To the degree that demographic subpopulations differ in their priorities and policy preferences, shifts in Illinois'population base are likely to have an impact on public opinion on several policy issues and priorities. It is, therefore, informative to understand the changing demography of the state and its connection to public opinion about various policy options.

Table 1 shows that the overall population of Illinois grew moderately between 1990 and 2003, increasing from 11.4 million in 1990 to 12.7 million in 2003 (an 11.1% increase). This chart also shows that the 1990s brought major change to the racial and ethnic composition of the Illinois' population. The population changes have not been evenly distributed in Illinois. The number of non-Hispanic whites decreased from 8.5 million in 1990 to 8.4 million by 2003. This represented a decrease of about 1.6%. In contrast, the number of Hispanic (non-black) residents increased from about 850,000 in 1990 to more than 1.7 million in 2003–an increase of more than 100%. The number of blacks in Illinois increased from 1.7 million in 1990 to 1.9 million in 2003. This represented an increase of 13%. The number of Asians and others also increased from just over 300,000 in 1990 to over 600,000 in 2003. This represents a 98% increase.

2

Table 1: Changes in Illinois' Racial Composition, 1990-2003

Race/ Ethnicity	1990		2003		1990-2003	
	Number	As % of Total	Number	As % of Total	Change	%Change
White (non-Hispanic)	8,556,289	74.9%	8,415,341	66.3%	-140,948	-1.6%
Black	1,707,405	14.9%	1,932,141	15.2%	169,470	13.2%
Hispanic (non-Black)	850,312	7.4%	1,726,822	13.6%	659,227	103.1%
Asian & Others	316,596	2.8%	627,719	4.9%	292,143	98.3%
Total	11,430,602	100.0%	12,702,023	100.0%	1,271,421	11.1%

Source: October 2003 Current Population Survey.

Table 1 also shows that in 1990, whites made up about 75% of Illinois'population. By 2003, they made up 66%. In 1990, blacks made up 14.9% of the Illinois population. By 2003, they made up 15.2% of the population. Hispanics made up 7.4% of the Illinois population in 1990, but by 2003, they made up 13.6%. Asians and others made up 2.8% of the Illinois population in 1990, but 4.9% by 2003.

Demographic shifts in the population are likely to have an impact on public opinion on several policy issues including levels of support for spending on education, job training, medical care, higher education, roads and highways, the environment, and support for low-income families, etc.

Each year, the Illinois Policy Survey (sponsored by Northern Illinois University) asks Illinois residents what they consider to be the most important problem facing the state (Peddle and Burrell, 2004). Figure 1 offers a historical perspective on the proportion of respondents who have identified certain major issues as the most important problem in Illinois since

Figure 1 :
The Most Important Issue Facing Illinois, 1992-2004

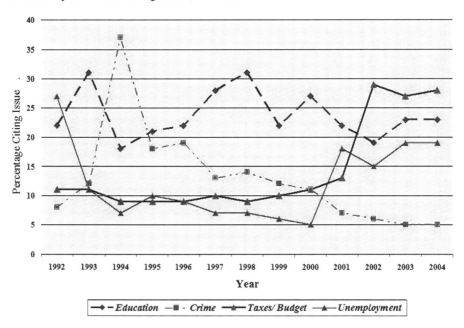

1992. From 1995 to 2001, responses to this question identified education as the most important problem, but since 2002, it has fallen to second place. Concerns about state spending and the state budget surpassed education concerns as the most important problem facing Illinois. Also, between 2002 and 2004, economic concerns such as unemployment have also risen to special prominence in the Illinois Policy Surveys. Concern over unemployment and jobs remains high, and concern over the state budget has grown substantially over the past few years.

One way we can gauge budgetary and economic concerns is by asking whether state spending for different major program areas should be increased, decreased, or remain the same. Figure 2 presents the results from the 2004 survey, which identifies the proportion of respondents who said that state government should increase spending for particular program areas. A majority of respondents supported increases in state spending for public

Figure 2: Percentage Favoring Increased Spending on Various Issues, 2004

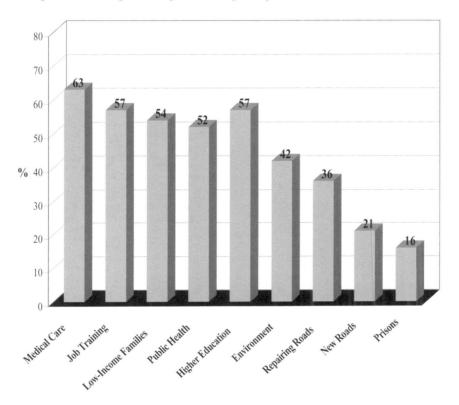

schools, medical care, public health, higher education, job training for the unemployed, and assistance for low income families.

Support for increases in state spending differs not only by the program area, but also by the characteristics of the respondent. The next diagram shows that residents of Chicago generally expressed greater support for increases in spending than did respondents from outside the city. More generally, respondents from Northern Illinois expressed greater support for increases in spending than did those in other areas of the state. And respondents from the Southern Illinois region generally expressed the lowest levels of support for increased spending.

Figure 3:
Percentage Favoring Increased Spending on Various Issues by Location, 2004

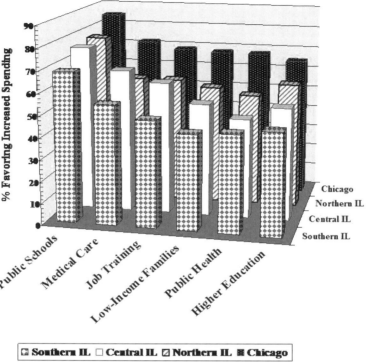

☐ Southern IL ☐ Central IL ☒ Northern IL ▩ Chicago

In general, Figure 4 shows that respondents who identified themselves as black or African American were more willing than other respondents to support increases in state spending, as were those respondents who identified themselves as Latino or Hispanic. Blacks (93%) and Hispanics (85%) were more likely than were whites (73%) to support more money for public schools. It also shows that African Americans (74%) and Hispanics (61%) were also more likely than whites (47%) to favor additional spending on medical care. This chart also shows that blacks (84%) and Hispanics (69%) were more likely than were whites (53%) to favor more spending for job training programs and additional spending on low-income families. The chart also illustrates that blacks and Hispanics were more likely than were whites to support additional funding for public health, as 82% of blacks, 79% of Hispanics, and 53% of whites support more funding in this

Figure 4:
Percentage Favoring Increased Spending on Various Issues by Race/Ethnicity, 2004

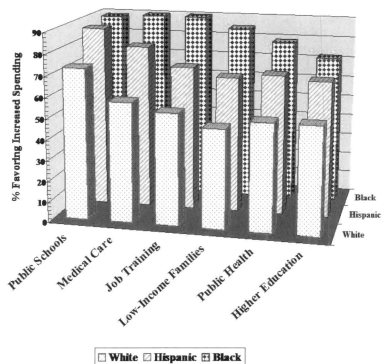

☐ **White** ☑ **Hispanic** ⊞ **Black**

area. Finally, blacks (76%) and Hispanics (82%) were also more likely than were whites (48%) to support more money for colleges and universities. Because the proportions of African Americans and Hispanics in Illinois have increased, their opinions are now weighted more heavily in the formulation of public opinion in the state.

Figures 5 and 6 show some other differences by respondent characteristics that are also notable. In general, support for increased state spending on each of the program areas declines as the income category of the respondent increases, but support for increased state spending on public schools was greatest among the lowest and highest income categories and remained high in all income categories. Party affiliation also mattered, with those respondents identifying themselves as Republicans being much less likely to support spending increases than Democrats or Independents.

Figure 5:
Percentage Favoring Increased Spending on Various Issues by Income, 2004

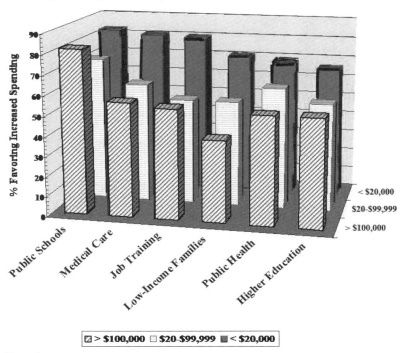

> $100,000 $20–$99,999   < $20,000

Figure 6:
Percentage Favoring Increased Spending on Various Issues by Party Identification, 2004

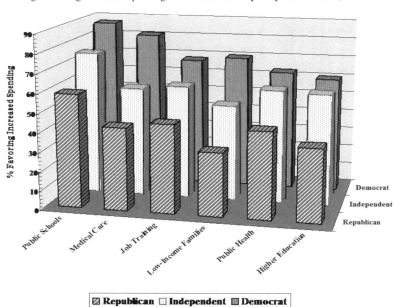

Republican   Independent   Democrat

When asked whether they favored or opposed using various measures to solve the state budget problems, respondents indicated varying levels of support for the different measures. Figure 7 shows that nearly two-thirds of respondents supported increasing corporate or business taxes as a means of solving the state budget problems, and slightly more than half of the respondents supported laying off government personnel. At the other extreme, only about one-third of respondents said that they would favor reductions in state services and only about one-quarter or less of respondents would favor increasing the state income tax or gasoline taxes as a means of solving the state's budget woes.

Figure 7:
Percentage Favoring Various Alternatives for Solving State Budget Problems, 2004

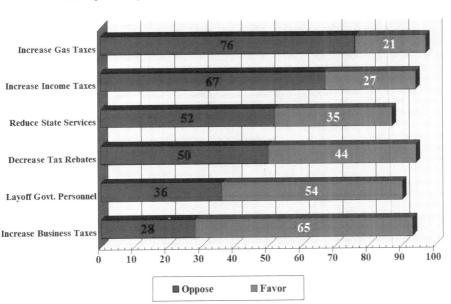

Finally, Figure 8 shows that the majority of respondents said that they would be willing to increase their taxes (by $25) to maintain service levels in each of nine different program areas. Public schools, medical care, temporary aid for needy families, and public health programs received the greatest support. Public safety, protecting open spaces, and public transportation programs received the lowest level of support. Still, more than half of residents endorsed the idea of maintaining spending levels for all of these items. But this is not true of all programs. Still, many of the respondents expressed a willingness to pay as much as $300 per year in additional state taxes to prevent service cuts and more than half were willing to pay at least $250 more in taxes to avoid cuts. The message sent by the respondents seems to be that cuts in spending are fine in the abstract and are preferred to tax increases, but they do not want service cuts to named programs even if it means paying more taxes to maintain service levels.

Figure 8:
Percentage Willing to Pay More to Maintain Service Program Levels, 2004

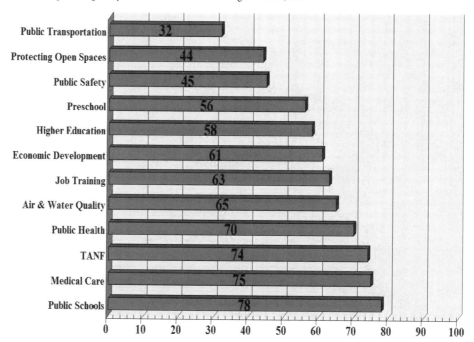

Overview of the Remaining Chapters

Demographic changes and public opinions are potentially important inputs into the public policy decision-making process. But they are not the only ones. The chapters that follow identify the role of additional factors that shape public policymaking in Illinois. In the next chapter, for example, Fred Giertz provides an insightful analysis of the Illinois state budget and the challenges facing the state over the next several years. He pays particular attention to the state's pension funding problem. He sugges ts that the state's budgetary problems are serious ones that offer no easy solutions. He cautions, however, that "focusing narrowly on pensions has led to inferior solutions to the state's underlying budget problem. . ." He suggests that while attempting to get its fiscal house in order, the state must avoid taking short-term budget measures that often worsen its longer term outlook.

Chapter 3, by Robert Rich and Chris Erb, offers an examination of critical health policy issues in Illinois and the nation. They suggest that Illinois is a microcosm for the nation as a whole, especially with respect to health care. Moreover, they suggest that Illinois is an innovator that has offered several bold proposals that may serve as models for the nation. Nevertheless, the state has not resolved tensions between increasing access and constraining costs. Rich and Erb suggest that these pressures will continue to dominate the health care reform debate in the state, and Illinois policymakers will face numerous important choices in the years to come. Noteworthy examples that they point to include figuring out how to pay for the Health Care Justice Act, the All Kids program, and new innovations in providing prescription drugs, especially as costs for these programs are projected to increase substantially in the next decade.

Naoko Muramatsu investigates long-term care in Illinois. She suggests that the long-term care system in Illinois faces several challenges: "the system of services is heavily biased toward nursing homes as opposed to the home and community settings; financing and delivery of services are fragmented and not very responsive to people's needs; and elders face limited access to needed services." As she notes, seniors and advocates are demanding changes to our long-term care system; the state budget faces unprecedented shortfalls and at the same time, legislators and state department leadership are beginning to acknowledge the need for reform. In moving forward on such reforms, she cautions against the inclination of relying on piecemeal strategies that parochially look only within the U.S. for models of what is possible. Rather, she points to some of the innovations from other countries, such as Germany and Japan, which have adopted approaches that assure access to long-term care for their residents, regardless of socioeconomic status.

In Chapter 5, Lorens Helmchen examines another dimension of health care: public financing of mental health and developmental disability services. This chapter clarifies the delicate balancing act the state must engage in to achieve its three goals with respect to delivering mental health and developmental disability services: (1) Grant access to care so that all people in need of services are able to obtain the services they desire. (2) Assure quality such that recipients receive a specified standard of care that results in a desired outcome. And (3) provide access and quality of care at minimum cost in an accountable fashion. As Helmchen suggests, when this balance is achieved and all three goals are met, they serve to "strengthen the confidence of patients, providers, and the public that tax revenues dedicated to serving this population are spent effectively and fairly."

Robert Rich and Cinthia Elkins discuss the state of children's health in Illinois. In doing so, they show how Illinois compares to other states in child health, child health insurance, and access to health care for children. They also describe current plans for making improvements in these areas. The chapter shows that Illinois falls close to the national average on several health status measures. Health disparities exist for Illinois children as they do for children in the rest of the nation. The chapter also discusses some of the recent changes and advances in providing health insurance to children such as KidCare. It shows that Illinois has been one of the leaders in expanding and improving children's health insurance programs in recent years. Rich and Elkins also examine the prospects for the All Kids program which would offer Illinois'uninsured children comprehensive health care . They conclude that Illinois is doing better than the nation as a whole with its recent improvements in children's health care.

Chapter 7, by Rachel Gordon and Elizabeth Powers, poses the question "Is there a shortage of child care in Illinois?" In addressing this question, they present an accessible analysis of what constitutes a shortage of child care, how such shortages can be measured, and what can be done when shortages exist. This critical analysis makes explicit some of the assumptions that underlie commonly held ideas. Gordon and Powers offer some less often discussed perspectives on these topics. In particular, they point out that when parents are responsible for paying the entire bill, they "are likely to spend more on center-based care for their young child than they would pay to send that child to college." Gordon and Powers argue that, despite evidence concerning the disadvantages of center-based (versus home-based care) for children's behavior and health, state policies continue to promote center-based care rather than weighing the positive benefits of home-based care. They believe that, at a minimum, the state should engage in systematic examination and evaluation of such policies.

In Chapter 8, Peter Mulhall asks "what are the best estimates for after-school needs based on the Illinois youth population and targeted risk conditions?" To address this central question, he suggests that we need a data driven approach that will give the most accurate estimates. This chapter, therefore, also asks, "what data sources are available to help define or estimate the need for after-school services in Illinois?" And "what are the strengths and limitations of these data sources and how should they be used to carefully guide the need-identification process at the state and local levels?" Mulhall argues that the need for after-school programs is contingent upon how one defines the family, child and community needs, and is based on the major goals and purposes of the after-school program. Few people doubt the need for after-school care for single-parent families living in poverty where fewer options are available because of the lack of resources. But there is also the possibility that even in two-parent families when both parents work, whether in poverty or not, children may need after-school services due to the significant amounts of unsupervised time when they may be hanging out with friends. He points out that time spent home alone is one of the critical factors related to high-risk problem behaviors. He concludes that priorities for determining need largely depend on whether policymakers view needs based on a universal population, targeted population, or education.

Madhu Khanna provides an analysis of the Conservation Reserve Enhancement Program (CREP) in Illinois in Chapter 9. Her essay examines the effectiveness of the Illinois CREP in achieving sediment abatement goals and the costs at which it has done so. It analyzes the design of the program and the criteria used to enroll land parcels and compares these to other alternative ways of targeting land parcels for enrollment to achieve the program goals at significantly lower costs. Khanna concludes with some policy implications for redesigning CREP in Illinois to improve program targeting and cost-effectiveness.

Kent Redfield tackles the topic of political corruption and ethics policy in Illinois in Chapter 10. After providing an overview of just how widespread and sordid political corruption has been Illinois over the last half century, he asks why. He offers the following explanation: Illinois' "political culture does little to attract good people to politics and even less to restrain the bad people who get into politics. And the political system we have developed in Illinois both reflects and reinforces the corruption of our political culture." He identifies several costs of corruption such as a loss of legitimacy for the political process, a decline in political participation, a weakening of the talent pool for public officials and those who work for government, and a deterioration of the quality of the public services that the state provides. On a more optimistic note, he offers some solutions. He recommends an effective gift ban law, placing more stringent limits and prohibitions on the role of money in Illinois politics through campaign finance reform, allowing only individuals to make contributions to political campaigns, and increasing the amount of information we have about public transactions and the private interests of public officials and public employees. In short, he argues that Illinois needs 'to raise public expectations about politics in order for Illinois politicians and citizens to reject the politics of personal and private interests and create a politics of the public interest and the common good."

In "The Information Technology Gender Gap," Mo-Yin Tam and Gilbert Bassett examine the gender gap in educational achievement and employment opportunities in information technology. They concentrate on the 'high-IT core" segment of the IT workforce where there has been the highest growth in employment and greatest increase in wages and salaries. Their results indicate that, while the gender gap in IT majors in colleges has narrowed over the years, it remains large. Moreover, the gap exists within all ethnic groups. Female students with the same math performance levels as males are less likely to become IT majors. In addition, while female students with stronger math performance are more likely to become IT majors, the impact of math performance is weaker for women. Their results show that closing the gender gap in math performance would only eliminate 14% of the technology gender gap.

In the final chapter, I examine how race and ethnicity are related to the digital divide and workforce readiness in Illinois. In particular, I show that Illinois is losing jobs in sectors that have the greatest percentage of racial and ethnic minorities at the same time that we are gaining jobs in sectors that have the smallest proportions of African Americans and Latinos. I point out that we continue to train racial minorities for occupations with decreasing labor demand at the same time that we do not sufficiently train them for jobs that are opening up in sectors that lack skilled workers. This pattern leads to a labor surplus at the same time that there is a skills shortage. I also link these trends to the digital divide and show that the technology gap is reinforced in schools, at home, and in the workplace. I discuss the implications of these trends for remaining competitive in the new digital economy. Finally, I briefly discuss some proposals that could help bridge the digital divide that occurs along racial and ethnic lines.

The State of the State of Illinois is a non-technical book that provides useful information about policy issues that are either currently on the state's agenda or on the horizon. We hope that you will use it as a resource and that it provides up-to-date information about current thinking and trends in policy issues that affect Illinois. We also hope that you will use it to become more familiar with some of the areas of expertise within the Institute of Government and Public Affairs at the University of Illinois. We believe this book is consistent with IGPA's history and mission of helping to improve public policies and the performance of government by disseminating research on public policy issues and the public decision-making process, and by facilitating the application of that research to the issues and problems confronting decision makers and others who address public issues. We hope you will agree.

References

Bureau of Labor Statistics. 2003. *October 2003 Current Population Survey (CPS) CPS Supplement Files*. Machine-Readable Electronic Data File.

Peddle, Michael T. and Barbara Burrell. 2004 *The 2004 Report on the Illinois Policy Survey.* DeKalb, IL: Northern Illinois University Center for Government Studies.

Chapter 2

The Illinois State Budget and Pensions[1]

J. Fred Giertz

Four years after the end of the recession that began in March 2001, the Illinois state budget is still seriously out of balance. Moreover, the state faces even more serious challenges in the near future when it must respond to increased demands for pension funding as well as the needs of a number of other state programs including the recently approved All Kids medical insurance for uninsured children. Rather than using the recovery period to get its fiscal house in order, the state has repeatedly temporized by using a number of short-term budget expedients. In this chapter, the budget problems of the state of Illinois that developed after the end of the stock market bubble in 2000 and after 9/11 will first be addressed. The state's response to these challenges will then be discussed with a special focus on pension issues. The chapter will conclude with an analysis of the challenges facing the state over the next several years, again with an in-depth analysis of the state's pension funding problem.

The Origins of the State Budget Problem

The state of Illinois along with most other state governments as well as the federal government entered the new century with extremely strong revenues and healthy budgets. Since the mid-1990s, an expanding economy with the run-up of stock market values and the attendant capital gains, stock options, and bonuses led to what in retrospect was a golden age of public finance. In his first term, President Clinton was pessimistic about the federal budget predicting "deficits as far as the eye could see." However, by the end of his second term, the federal government was running a surplus for the first time in 30 years with projections for continued surpluses far into the future.

Talk then turned to what might happen if the federal government paid off its debt.

Similarly, states including Illinois were suddenly experiencing large and unexpected surges in revenue each year. Further, some of their spending problems that had dogged states also appeared to recede. For example, welfare case loads declined after the approval of welfare reform measures in 1996 and with the strong economy. Medical care cost inflation was relatively moderate during this period, constrained by the widespread adoption of managed care plans. Finally, lingering pension funding problems for states were eased by the impact of the stock market appreciation on pension assets. States such as Illinois even accumulated relatively large fund balances from the windfall revenues.

Circumstances changed quickly after the end of the stock market bubble and the beginning of the 2001 recession. Suddenly, the federal government was again facing deficits as far as the eye could see and most states were experiencing unprecedented drops in revenue. The steep run-up of tax revenues on the up side was followed by an even sharper drop. In the past in Illinois, politicians generally considered it a crisis when tax revenues grew, but increased less rapidly than the rate of inflation. The fiscal problems facing the state in fiscal 2002 through 2004 were far worse that any experienced in recent memory, at least since the Great Depression.

The Illinois had state general fund revenues of $24.1 billion in FY2001 and revenues were expected to grow to $25 billion in FY2002. Instead, revenues plummeted to $23.4 billion, a decline of 3 percent and $1.7 billion below expectations. This was followed by another revenue decline of 2.5 percent in FY2003. In real terms, state revenues fell by more than 9 percent in this two-year period, far beyond what anyone currently serving in government had ever encountered.

This decline in revenue did not elicit an immediate response of spending austerity during the last years of the Ryan administration. Initially, most observers believed that the downturn in revenues would not last very long since the national recession in 2001 was relatively mild. Further, the state had substantial general fund balances that were used to buffer in revenue decline early on.

When Rod Blagojevich (D) became governor in January 2003 midway through the second rough budget year, the state faced a major budget imbalance since there had been few permanent spending cuts to offset the severe revenue declines. The new administration had to find a way to deal with the problem. The obvious answer was to raise taxes and/or to cut spending. However, the governor's options were very limited in this regard given his campaign promises that were renewed after he was elected. First he promised no major tax increases: "If the legislature sends me a budget that raises the income tax or the sales tax, I will veto it." This was accompanied by another pledge on the spending side: "If the legislature sends me a budget that cuts K-12 education, healthcare or public safety I will veto that too." The governor, in effect, put the state's two largest funding sources off limits for tax increases and promised not to cut the state's three largest spending categories.

The Response of the Blagojevich Administration

Given the severity of the budget crises and the governor's self-imposed constraints, the governor faced a daunting fiscal challenge. The challenge was met with a series of bold and innovative measures that focused on getting the state through its short-term woes while avoiding the longer term issues. In fact, the short-term budget measures often worsened the longer term outlook. To the extent that spending was maintained through the use of one-time, non-recurring revenue sources or through pushing the costs into the future by borrowing, the short-term measures made longer term solutions more difficult.

Seldom is a blueprint laid out as clearly as the ones used by the Blagojevich administration. In early 2003, Ronald Picur, a professor of accounting and finance at the University of Illinois at Chicago and director of the Center for Governmental Accounting Research and Education, and an associate published an article in the journal *Government Finance Review* (April 2003)[2] detailing strategies whose use "undermines long-term financial stability and citizen confidence in government." These strategies were labeled "worst practices," that should be avoided so "governments are steered in the direction of the tougher policy choices that are needed to address situations of budgetary stress." The list of worst practices included:

o One-time revenue sources to meet continuing expenditure demands
o Non-general fund infusions into the general fund
o Pension obligation bonds
o Asset sales and leasebacks

This is a list of practices that most budget experts would agree should be avoided.

About this same time, Professor Picur went to work as a consultant for the Blagojevich's Office of Management and Budget, headed by John Filan, who was a former Picur associate in an accounting firm. According to published reports, Picur received nearly $300,000 in consulting fees from the state and also served on the governor's Budget Advisory Panel.

Ironically, the first actions proposed by the Blagojevich administration were virtually identical to the "worst practices" cited above. In addition to raising a number of business fees, the governor's first Illinois budget relied heavily on one-time revenue sources to close the budget gap. This included a $10 billion borrowing plan to fund the state's public pension systems that were and still are seriously underfunded. In one sense, the pension borrowing plan was an astute arbitrage play on the part of the state, borrowing at a low long-term interest rate and then investing the proceeds in the various pension portfolios where the expected long-term return was much higher. However, instead of using expected gains to deal with long-term funding issues, the $2.2 billion hoped for a windfall went to replace pension fund payments scheduled to be made from generals funds for the remainder of FY2003 and 2004.[3] The expected savings were all applied immediately to help fill the budget gap. In retrospect, this gave the state two years of breathing room before the next pension funding crisis arose.

Not all the strategies proposed in the budget were approved, such as sale of assets including the Thompson Center, the state's Chicago office building. This was a proposed sale and leaseback arrangement that was expected to yield $200 million for the state. The governor's first budget also called for the auctioning off of the state's tenth riverboat casino license, which never occurred because of an array of legal issues in transferring the license. The state did make intensive use of shifting non-general fund balances including some from the road fund into the state's general fund to support current spending, making use of one-time revenues to fund ongoing expenditure needs.

Many of these strategies could have been justified as temporary measures that were needed while the state was getting its fiscal house in order. Even borrowing could have been used productively to give state time to make the painful adjustments necessary to return to long-term balance. In Illinois, however, these techniques were used, not to restore stability, but to support spending increases that could not be financed with long-term, stable revenue sources. What might have been a stabilizing policy actually contributed to instability in the long term.

The Myth of a Balanced State Budget

There is a general belief that states such as Illinois must operate with a balanced budget while the federal government has the ability, for good or for ill, to operate with deficit financing. The Illinois Constitution states in the Finance Article (Article VII, section 2):

> The Governor shall prepare and submit to the General Assembly, at a time prescribed by law, a State budget for the ensuing fiscal year. . . . Proposed expenditures shall not exceed funds estimated to be available for the fiscal year as shown in the budget.

Note that the so-called balanced budget requirement is strictly prospective in the sense that proposed revenues shall not exceed the expected revenue with the revenue estimates provided by the governor. Former budget director Stephen Schnorf paraphrased this by saying that the Illinois budget needs to be balanced only one day of the year, the day of the governor's budget address, with the governor acting as score keeper.

Further, the state constitution does not require that expenditures be

20

covered by current revenues from taxes and other traditional sources such as fees and charges. Borrowed funds count toward the balance as do planned pension underfunding arrangements. If such rules were used at the federal level, the federal budget would always be balanced since deficits created by imbalances between expenditures and tax receipts are always covered by the issuance of federal debt.

If the balanced budget myth was ever believed in Illinois, this belief clearly has ended during the last three years. By any traditional measures, Illinois'budget has been out of balance in both the short run and, even more seriously, over the long run where a substantial structural deficit looms in the future. A structural deficit is the difference between the expected future expenditures required to maintain existing levels of state services and the future revenues that will be generated by the existing tax and fee structure.

The Death of Transparency

Along with the new administration's innovative financing techniques, fiscal information became increasingly difficult to acquire, making budget analysis considerably more challenging. Until 2003, the Illinois Bureau of the Budget (BOB), which was renamed the Office of Management and Budget (OMB) in 2003 under the new administration, prepared a document at the beginning of each fiscal year that summarized the results of the last fiscal year and incorporated the revenue forecasts on which the new budget, as approved by the General Assembly, was predicated. For example, the BOB issued a report entitled "End of Fiscal Year 2002 Financial Report" in July 2002. This document provided a framework for evaluating state revenues on a month-by-month basis as the fiscal year progressed.

In the last three budget cycles, no similar document has been produced by the OMB. The state of Illinois' recent budgets are without doubt the most complex and challenging fiscal plans the state has ever adopted. There have been a multitude of new revenue sources including new taxes and fees, innovative borrowing plans, the proposed sale of state assets, and transfers among the state's various funds. The revenue estimates for these new sources as well as the forecasts for continuing revenue sources have not been made available publicly. For example, in 2003 there was no formal accounting of how the $700 million in additional aid from the federal government that was approved as part of the recent federal bill cutting taxes was to be used. Moreover, the "Quarterly Financial Report" (a quarterly update of state finances) no longer contains information about actual state revenue performance compared to expectations. The only published budget documents about revenue forecasts are the governor's budget submissions to the Illinois General Assembly each year. However, the budgets that have been actually approved are usually markedly different in many respects from the ones submitted by the governor.

The result of this information blackout has been the source of consternation for various state agencies and nongovernmental budget analysts. There is great concern about whether the state is meeting its fiscal targets and what the budget picture will be like in future years. Without a basic budget framework, these issues are almost impossible to analyze.

In response to the information vacuum, the Commission on Government Forecasting and Accountability (formerly Economic and Fiscal Commission), a legislative commission in some ways similar to the federal Congressional Budget Office, produces a document each year after the budget is adopted that attempts to incorporate the state's budget actions into a comprehensible framework that can be used to follow budget developments as the fiscal year unfolds. While this document is extremely valuable, it lacks the official status of OMB releases.

Recent Developments

The budget for fiscal 2006 that was approved in the spring of 2005 was dominated by state pension funding issues. Past governors and the General Assemblies have made ample use of pension funding maneuvers to provide temporary budget relief to the detriment of long-term fiscal stability. This has resulted in the various Illinois state pension systems being among the most poorly funded in the nation. In his FY2006 budget address, Blagojevich focused squarely on the state's pension problems, blaming them for much of the broader fiscal problems and suggesting cuts as a means of addressing these problems. He neglected to mention, however, pensions are more a manifestation of the state's problems rather than the root cause of these problems and more comprehensive changes must be made beyond pension cuts for the state to return to fiscal balance.

The governor suggested that the state pension problem was the result of overly generous benefits bestowed in a haphazard way by past General Assemblies and governors. In fact, the so-called pension problem should be viewed as a more general state budget problem that manifests itself in high pension costs because the state's pension systems have been used in the past to mask more basic budget issues. On many occasions in the last several decades, maneuvers involving the state's pension systems have been used to avoid painful political choices of raising either taxes or cutting state programs.

The heart of the current pension problem is the long-term under-funding of the state's pension systems where funds that should have gone for pensions have been used for other state programs. Each year, actuaries for the pension systems calculate the normal costs of the systems—the increased liabilities for promised future benefits created in that year. If the contributions of the state and the employees equal this normal cost, the pension systems will remain fully funded, assuming the actuarial assumptions are met.

From their inception, the state has almost always chosen to fund pensions at less than their normal cost, thus creating unfunded liabilities that have to be made up in the future. This was done explicitly during the austere budget days of the 1980s when Gov. Thompson and the General Assembly chose to direct the available state resources to other state programs and underfund the pensions. This was not an oversight, but a conscious policy decision. A case can be made to underfund pensions during lean times with the shortfall made up during the good years. In Illinois' case, every year was a lean year and the shortfalls were never made up. Unfortunately for the state, the underfunding was not invested in the portfolios of the pension systems and therefore missed out on the phenomenal growth in the financial markets from the early 1980s through the end of the century. Simulations for the State Universities Retirement System indicate that, had the state made its required contributions along with the contributions mandated for employees (which were made), the system would be fully funded at the end of fiscal 2004 with assets at nearly 110 percent of accrued liabilities even after the decline of the stock market after 2000 and the state would only have to contribute its share of the normal pension costs in the future-a fraction of the costs they now face.

In 1995, the state of Illinois realized the seriousness of the under-funding problem and set out on a course to correct it. It is safe to say the state did not act precipitously in this regard. In fact, the state adopted a 50-year plan to bring the various pension systems up to a modest goal of 90 percent of full funding. Not only did the plan stretch the catch-up over half a century, it delayed any real catching up for 15 years. The period from 1995 to 2010 was labeled a ramp phase in which the state still contributed less than the normal cost of annual pension liability increases with the serious business of making up the past underfunded liability deferred at 15 years. While the 1995 plan was a step in the right direction, it was like an overweight person deciding to go on a diet, but delaying any reduction in calorie consumption until 15 years in the future. Thus, the impending avalanche alluded to by the governor is one that every informed policy-maker has known about for at least a decade. With properly funded pension systems, the state would not be facing these quantum increases in funding levels mandated over the next several years.

Note that if the state had dealt with its past budget problems by issuing bonds in the credit market rather than by underfunding pensions, the state would now have a bond repayment problem, not a pension problem. In such a case, would the appropriate policy be to default on the bonds?

Since the pension funding reform in 1995, it is alleged that the pension systems have provided generous benefit increases and early retirement options. In one sense, there is an element of truth in these statements, but these changes have, for the most part, been instigated by the state in order to save money in other programs. For example, there was an increase in the retirement benefit formula for those retiring under defined benefit plans approved in 1997. However, the increased benefits came at a cost. As a kind of quid pro quo, the state eliminated a costly program that paid state employees for a portion of their unused sick leave at retirement while also tightening the eligibility requirements for state-subsidized medical insurance for retirees. The state captured the savings in the form of lower general fund spending while the costs were borne by increases in the unfunded liability of the pension system.

In another case, certain state workers gave up a scheduled pay increase in return for the state picking up a larger portion of their retirement contributions. Here again, the state saved the forgone wage costs while the burden was placed on the retirement systems.

Finally, early retirement programs, that have become common in recent years, are portrayed as costly benefits for young retirees. While a strong case can be made for limiting early retirements and possibly raising the retirement age, most early retirement programs were designed to help the state and school districts by moving older workers out of their jobs and into retirement. Again the state and the schools capture the benefits of lower wage costs while the pension systems bear the burden of increased underfunding. It is interesting to note that when officials bemoan the increased underfunding of the pension systems from early retirements, they seldom mention the offsetting savings in payroll and fringe benefits resulting from the early retirements.

In response to the growing pension costs, the governor proposed and the General Assembly approved cutbacks in state pensions. However, the state was severely limited in its ability to reduce the currently-accrued pension liabilities by Article XII, Section 5 of the State Constitution. The so-called non-impairment clause states:

> Membership in any pension or retirement system of the State, any unit of local government or school district, or any agency or instrumentality thereof, shall be an enforceable contractual relationship, the benefits of which shall not be diminished or impaired.

As a consequence, most of the pension changes applied to new, not existing employees (including downstate teachers).[4] The problem with the new pension changes is that they save the state money years (often decades) in the future, yet these benefits are counted as revenue in the current year's budget. In a sense, this is business as usual where pensions are used as a device to defer costs into the future with the state still facing yet another pension funding crisis several years in the future when pension costs are scheduled to increase sharply.

The Future

The so-called FY2006 pension reforms "save" the state $2.2 billion in pension contributions during the current and upcoming fiscal years at the expense of substantial extra costs in the out years. In reality, the state's pension problems have not been solved, but merely moved forward a few years. Under the new plan, state pension contributions are scheduled to increase by $613 million in FY2008, $661 in FY2009, and $709 million in FY2010.[5] In four years, there still will be the requirement to contribute $2.4 billion more to pensions than is being paid this year. This additional contribution will approach 8 percent of the state budget, probably more than all the expected annual revenue growth during this period. In other words, the state would have to devote virtually all of its new revenues over the next several years to nothing but pensions. This is clearly an impossibility given other state needs and commitments.

As noted above, the state has a structural budget imbalance problem, not just a pension problem, even though pension costs have come to play an important role in both the problem and its solution. The problem is a serious one and the solutions are not easy. The solutions require a comprehensive review of state expenditures and revenues. Focusing narrowly on pensions has led to inferior solutions to the state's underlying budget problem that will not be sustainable in even the near term of 5 to 10 years. Soon, the state of Illinois must face the prospect of either making large and painful cuts in major state programs (not just cuts in pension benefits decades in the future) or finding additional permanent revenue sources to fund its activities.

Notes

[1] Some of the material in this chapter is drawn from articles written in the last three years by the author that have appeared in *State Tax Notes*, and the *National Tax Journal*. This piece uses considerable material that has been updated, from the author's guest essay in the April 2005 *Illinois Issues* entitled "Cause as Solution."

[2] Rowan A. Miranda and Ronald D. Picur, "CFO as Budget Magician: Fiscal Illusion in Public Finance," *Government Finance Review*, April 2003.

[3] The remainder of the funds will be placed with the pension systems to be invested with the hope that the expected investment returns of 8 percent or more will exceed the state's borrowing costs, estimated at 6 percent or less. The success of this arbitrage play obviously depends on the performance of pension fund investments. In any case, the state was forced to make pension fund contributions estimated at $2 billion from general fund revenues beginning in FY2005.

[4] The plan that was approved also contained a provision designed to reduce the practice of artificially inflating end-of-career salary increases to increase pension benefits. The granting institution will now have to pay the increased pension costs for raises of about 4 percent during the final years of service. This provision has merit although the 6 percent limit may be overly restrictive, especially if inflation rates increase in the future.

[5] These estimates were taken from a Deloitte report based on submissions of the actuaries for the state's various pension funds.

Chapter 3

State of the State of Health Care in Illinois in 2006

Robert F. Rich and Christopher T. Erb

Introduction to Health Care Issues Facing Illinois in 2006

Illinois is a microcosm of the United States on a number of critical health care policy issues. We face many of the same policy challenges that are being addressed at the national level including access to health care for the growing number of uninsured adults and children and cost containment. Moreover, Illinois has recently been at center stage of several important national controversies in health care policy, including the issue of prescription drug importation, medical malpractice reform, Medicaid financing reform, and managed care legal liability.

Over the past decade, Illinois has led reform efforts in some of these areas, and has lagged behind reform trends in other areas. Most recently, however, Illinois has been in the vanguard, pushing reform on prescription drug pricing and efforts to reduce the number of uninsured children and adults. Current initiatives underway in the state include one that would expand Medicaid coverage to all children in the state, and another that seeks strategies to ensure that all Illinois residents have adequate health care coverage. While these plans have been controversial, they position Illinois as a major player in health care reform nationally.

The health care system in Illinois has evolved over time in response to a series of strong tensions and even contradictions. This is because there are competing priorities for Illinois policymakers with regard to health care programs which are publicly funded. On the one hand, rising costs are straining state budgets and they must be controlled. On the other hand, Governor Blagojevich has made it a priority of his administration to increase access to health care for children and adults in the state. These tensions reflect the fact that there is little societal consensus on critical questions of health care policy. However, this may be changing in Illinois based on the recent passage of Governor Blagojevich's All Kids program and the Health Care Justice Act.

Some of the recent proposals in Illinois seek to change the underlying assumptions about the nature of the role of government in the health care system. The Health Care Justice Act, which was passed in 2004, challenges the assumption that access to health care is not a legal right of citizenship for Americans. At the same time, Illinois has become more receptive to the use of managed care arrangements in its public health care programs, a step it resisted during the 1990s when many other states were pioneering managed care initiatives in Medicaid and other public programs.

Illinois also is experiencing tensions similar to those seen across the country. In this chapter, we explore some of the major issues in Illinois and outline the most recent reform initiatives underway in the state. Included in this overview is the state's Medicaid program and recent initiatives to expand coverage. We review Illinois' experienc e with managed care in its public programs, including discussion of two Supreme Court cases that began in Illinois dealing with the issue of legal liability for managed care organizations. We also briefly review two other areas in which Illinois has recently been in the national spotlight: prescription drugs and medical mal-practice reform.

Health Care Problems Facing Illinois
Rates of Insurance Coverage

A major health care issue facing the nation, as a whole, is access to the health care service delivery system. In 2004, of the 293 million people in the US, 16% were uninsured, 12% covered by Medicare, 13% were covered by Medicaid, 5% had individually-purchased private coverage, and 54% had employer-provided private coverage (Kaiser Family Foundation, 2005). Participation in employer-sponsored health care coverage dropped from 67%

to 63% between 2001 and 2003, which has been a major contributor to the rise in the number of uninsured Americans, and at least part of the reason for the 40% increase in Medicaid caseloads nationwide (National Governors' Association, 2005). This reflected a general decrease in private health insurance coverage and increase in public coverage during the past five years (Employee Benefits Research Institute, 2004).

Insurance Coverage in Illinois

In comparison with the national data above, in 2004, of Illinois' 12,713,634 residents, 14% (1,790,840) were uninsured, 21% (2.7 million) had either Medicare (12%) or Medicaid (9%), and 63% had private insurance. Of the privately insured, 7.3 million (57%) had employer-sponsored insurance and 623,650 (5%) had individual health insurance coverage (Kaiser Family Foundation, 2005). Illinois ranked 5th of all states for total numbers of Medicaid beneficiaries, but 41st on the percentage of residents covered by that program. Illinois ranked 23rd of all states in terms of the number of uninsured residents in the state. Among states in the mid-west, Illinois had the highest percentage of uninsured and the lowest percentage of people enrolled in Medicaid in 2003-04 (Kaiser Family Foundation, 2005).

Approximately 14% of the population in Illinois lacks health insurance. The health consequences of being uninsured are serious, leading to more illness and avoidable health problems. The uninsured are more likely than those with insurance to be hospitalized for conditions that could have been avoided (Kaiser Family Foundation, 2003). Addressing the problem of the uninsured will require multi-faceted reforms that, in addition to expanding public insurance coverage options, also encourage employer offering and employee uptake of health insurance benefits. Many states have developed proposals to encourage uptake of employee health benefits, including tax credits for individuals and businesses. In 2005, legislatures in 19 states have considered proposals to expand coverage. For example, California, Minnesota, and New York are considering bills that would create universal health insurance programs for all state residents, and Massachusetts is about to pass a bill that would require all state residents to purchase health insurance (*USA Today*, July 9, 2005, page 5B). The Vermont legislature recently passed a measure providing universal, publicly-funded health coverage. In Illinois, the current proposal to expand coverage to all residents–The Health Care Justice Act–is multifaceted, and encourages increased coverage on a number of fronts using various strategies.

On July 1, 2004, the General Assembly of the State of Illinois passed The Health Care Justice Act (Public Act 093-0973), in which it stated that "It is a policy goal of the State of Illinois to insure that all residents have access to quality health care at costs that are affordable." The Act provides that "the State of Illinois is strongly encouraged to implement a health care access plan that does the following: (1) provides access to a full range of preventive, acute, and long-term health care services; (2) maintains and improves the quality of health care services offered to Illinois residents; (3) provides portability of coverage, regardless of employment status; (4) provides core benefits for all Illinois residents; (5) encourages regional and local consumer participation; (6) contains cost-containment measures; (7) provides a mechanism for reviewing and implementing multiple approaches to preventive medicine based on new technologies; and (8) promotes affordable coverage options for the small business market. The Act also created the "Adequate Health Care Task Force," which has been charged with developing elements of a plan to solve the problem of the uninsured and underinsured in Illinois.

The Adequate Health Care Task Force faces some critical challenges, if the experiences of other states that have proposed large expansions of public health insurance coverage are to serve as examples. Between 1989 and 1993, Florida, Hawaii, Massachusetts, Minnesota, Oregon, and Washington all adopted statutes that would provide some form of universal coverage to all state residents within a decade. Washington, for example, adopted an employer mandate in which employers had the option to operate their own plan, contract with another plan, purchase their own health care plan, or join a "health care purchasing cooperative" (Weissert and Weissert, 1996: 231-232). Other states that stopped short of universal coverage proposals nonetheless adopted elements of some of the more comprehensive initiatives, including small group insurance regulation reform, which would make it easier for small businesses to insure their employees at affordable prices, experiments with new service delivery systems such as the competitive bid fixed-price arrangements for Medicaid clients used in Arizona, and creating home and community-based long-term care programs for the elderly, such as in New York and Connecticut (Weissert and Weissert, 1996: 216-217). However, Washington and Oregon's more comprehensive plans were later repealed, and the Massachusetts plan was never implemented (Holahan and Nichols, 1996: 39). And more recently in Vermont, Governor Jim Douglas vetoed the bill that would have created a state-operated comprehensive health insurance program for all Vermont residents, citing concerns that the program would result in fewer choices, fewer benefits, and fewer health care providers in the state (Parnell, 2005).

Whether Illinois' experience with expanding coverage under the Health Care Justice Act will become a model for health care reform in other states depends on how successful the state is in building coalitions of support for the program. If this "experiment" is successful, it may provide an example for other states to follow if and when they are ready to attempt broad health care reform initiatives.

Illinois has also been a leader in expanding coverage for children, and in August 2005, Governor Blagojevich decided to make covering children among his highest health care reform priorities, introducing a plan to cover all children in Illinois, regardless of their family's income, within the next five years. The Governor recently garnered enough support for his "All Kids" proposal to pass it into law in October 2005, and he signed the final version of the bill on November 15 (Office of the Governor Press Release, November 15, 2005).

Currently about 10% of children in Illinois are uninsured, with rates significantly higher (up to 15%) in urban areas, and somewhat lower (about 7%) in rural areas. The All Kids program is projected to cover 253,000 Illinois children who currently have no health insurance (Office of the Governor Press Release, October 27, 2005). Under the proposal, uninsured children would have access to doctor's visits, hospital stays, vision, dental and hearing care, and prescription drugs. Their parents would pay a premium based on their income, with no income cap. Any child who has been uninsured for 12 months would be eligible, but the parents' premium contribution would vary depending on their income. Parents who earn in the income range of $40,000 to $59,000 would pay a monthly premium of $40 per child, with a maximum of $80. Parents whose income is $60,000 to $79,000 would pay a monthly premium of $70 per child, and no more than $140 total per family (Aquilar, 2005).

It is expected that this plan would be paid for by the savings resulting from switching these children to a managed care plan, in which each patient would have a "primary care case manager" instead of randomly visiting doctors, clinics, and emergency rooms. The projected savings of $45 million in the first year would cover approximately 50,000 children, and five years into the program, all the state's uninsured children would be covered (Office of the Governor Press Release, October 27, 2005).

The program would be structured as a Primary Care Case Management (PCCM) arrangement. The proposed PCCM program would be a state Medicaid agency-controlled managed care plan in which the savings generated from increased efficiency and better coordination of care would be funneled back into the Medicaid program. These programs are designed to contain costs by streamlining care for those enrolled, and more than 25 other states are in the process of implementing primary care case management and disease management programs for their Medicaid populations (Rosenbaum et al., 2002).

In a year when many states are freezing eligibility and enrollment expansions for their Medicaid programs, the All Kids program represents a bold statement that Illinois is committed to addressing the health care needs of children and their families.

Medicaid Coverage and Costs

Nationally, Medicaid pays for about one-sixth of all health care expenditures and half of all nursing home care. It covers 39 million low-income people and 13 million elderly and people with disabilities. The

Medicaid program provides health insurance coverage for low-income individuals and families, additional assistance to low-income Medicare beneficiaries, long-term care (LTC) coverage, including LTC insurance and nursing home care, and general support for the health care safety net, including public hospitals and clinics (Center for Medicare and Medicaid Services, 2003).

Medicaid is a federal-state partnership, and it represents the single largest federal grant to the states—42% of all federal grants to states. Total Medicaid expenditures for the nation were $288 billion in 2004, and in 2005 Medicaid expenditures are expected to rise to $329 billion nationally (National Governors' Association, 2005). In the current economic environ-ment, states are faced with serious revenue shortfalls and are looking for ways to cut, freeze, and restrict spending in their Medicaid and SCHIP budgets, which now comprise, on average, 15% of their total state budgets.

One way that states have dealt with the issue of rising costs is to experiment with innovative ways of providing Medicaid services through various mechanisms, such as managed care. These experiments require waivers from federal Medicaid regulations. Medicaid waivers provide a mechanism for many states to expand coverage to "optional" groups of people or to experiment with pilot projects. Waivers permit states to receive federal Medicaid funds for expenditures not otherwise allowed by federal law. Other states have found these waivers to be useful in allowing them to expand coverage to more potential Medicaid beneficiaries while still being able to control the overall costs of the program. For the most part, Illinois has not taken advantage of the Medicaid Managed Care waiver programs, and where it has done so Illinoisans who are eligible for Medicaid have been slow to adopt this option.

Medicaid and Rising Costs in Illinois

Illinois' Medicaid program covers over 1.7 million low-income individuals in the state—this is nearly 1 in 7 Illinoisans, or 13.5% of the population. In 2004, Illinois ranked 7th in terms of total Medicaid expenditures with just over $10 billion, and 6th in terms of the state-contributed portion of expenditures at $5.034 billion (2003 data). It was ranked 20th in terms of its Medicaid payments per enrollee at \$4,531 in 2001 (Kaiser Family Foundation, 2005). The program pays for almost 40% of all births in the state and 20% of all children. It covers 50% of nursing home costs and 50% of the costs of caring for people with HIV/AIDS. It covers most public expenditures for mental health care in the state, and it funds "safety net" hospitals that provide care to low-income citizens. In 2004, \$6.4 billion went to acute care services, \$3.2 billion went for long-term care services, and \$379 million went to safety net hospitals (Kaiser Family Foundation, 2005).

Illinois is in the lowest bracket of matching federal funds, receiving 50% of its total expenditures from the federal government. Medicaid currently accounts for 22.5% of total state expenditures, a figure that has more than doubled since 1992. Between 2000 and 2001, state expenditures for Medicaid increased by 12.2% and in 2002 another 13% increase in total state expenditures was recorded. These increases outstripped increases in state tax revenues by more than 10%, and were in range of the national Medicaid cost increases of 10.6% and 12.7% for those years (Kaiser Family Foundation, 2005). Since 2004, state Medicaid budget growth has outpaced total state budget growth by an average of over 7.0% (NASBO, 2005).

As a result of this rapid growth in Medicaid expenditures, many states developed plans to cut provider reimbursement rates in 2005-06, including hospitals, physicians, nursing homes, and even managed care firms (Kaiser Commission on Medicaid and the Uninsured, 2005). In Illinois, however, such a plan is likely to be heavily resisted by providers, as Medicaid providers are already concerned that Illinois has a current reimbursement backlog of \$1 billion. On October 17, 2005, the State announced a plan to borrow the \$1 billion and begin paying its Medicaid bills immediately (Illinois Hospital Association, 2005). This should help stem opposition from some provider groups and make providers more willing to accept coverage expansion proposals, such as the All Kids program (Parsons and Graham, 2005).

While Medicaid reimbursement rates tend to remain below rates in the private sector, they are, nonetheless, on the rise. For example, in 1998

Illinois spent $4,574 per enrollee–$6.7 billion total. This represented 14.8% of Illinois' total personal health care spending, an inc rease from 9.1% in 1991. The average annual increase of Medicaid spending in Illinois between 1991 and 2001 was 11% (Kaiser Family Foundation, 2005). This has created a crisis for states that are under extreme financial pressures and have sought strategies to deal with the cost pressures of Medicaid. The Center for Medicare and Medicaid Services (CMS) has encouraged innovative initiatives that states have proposed, and has created a number of waiver programs to allow states to experiment with different arrangements in their Medicaid programs.[1]

Illinois has taken greatest advantage of waivers under the Health Insurance Flexibility and Accountability (HIFA) Demonstration Initiative, which allows states to increase the number of individuals with health insurance coverage within current-level Medicaid and SCHIP resources. They are targeted toward populations with incomes below 200% of Federal Poverty Level (FPL), and emphasize strategies that utilize private health insurance coverage options.[2] With these waivers, states can expand coverage within existing resources and through employer-based initiatives. Alternatively, many states, prompted by current state fiscal pressures, are seeking HIFA waivers to reduce benefits, increase beneficiary cost sharing, and cap enrollment in ways that may not be otherwise permitted under federal law.

In 2002, Illinois received a waiver under this program, for its "KidCare Parent Coverage Demonstration." This is Illinois' proposal to provide combined coverage for low income children under Medicaid and SCHIP. The program provides coverage primarily of parents of children enrolled in Medicaid and the SCHIP. In an effort to de-stigmatize participation in this program, Illinois decided to call all coverage for children under this waiver "KidCare." Illinois enrolled more than 83,000 children in KidCare in 2001 and another 68,000 in 2002. From the end of the fiscal year 2002 through fiscal year 2003, the number of children covered by KidCare grew from 75,302 to 85,642, an increase of nearly 14%. Overall more than 750,000 children and pregnant women have been enrolled through aggressive outreach efforts throughout the state (Center for Medicare and Medicaid Services, 2004).

Illinois also introduced FamilyCare as part of its HIFA waiver initiative. Beginning in October 2002, FamilyCare expanded medical coverage for parents of low-income children. Later in fiscal year 2003, two additional expansions of eligibility were implemented, one for parents and one for children, to capture a larger population. FamilyCare provides a full range of health benefits to eligible children, 18 years of age and younger, and their parents. To be eligible, children with countable family income between 185% and 200% of the FPL and parents with countable family income between 49% and 90% of the FPL ($1,380 per month for a family of four) are now eligible for KidCare and FamilyCare. At the end of 2003, 1,286,521 children and their parents were covered by one of six KidCare and FamilyCare plans (Center for Medicare and Medicaid Services, 2004).

Managed Care

As of June 2004, overall enrollment in managed care plans nationally had settled at about 177.8 million (Managed Care National Statistics, 2005). Of the 44.4 million Medicaid beneficiaries in the country at that time, 22.9 million were enrolled in managed care plans, which was roughly 61% of total Medicaid enrollment nationally. This represented an increase of Medicaid managed care enrollment from only 13.3 million (40.1%) in 1996 (CMS, Medicaid Managed Care, 2005).

In the private sector, Managed Care Organizations (MCOs) have demonstrated an ability to control utilization and slow the rate of growth in utilization, which resulted in a slowing of insurance premium increases. In the 1990s growth of managed care coincided with a sharp reduction in the growth of health care costs. National data from that period suggest that managed care organizations were substantially more efficient than traditional indemnity plans in controlling costs (Rosenbaum and Kamoie, 2002). Furthermore, the available evidence suggests that there has not been a reduction in the quality of care provided under managed care, even in areas that have been specifically targeted for regulation, such as maternity care. While the evidence about the quality of care provided under managed care has been mixed, analyses reviewing over 100 primary studies have found nearly equal numbers of examples of managed care arrangements that increased quality as those that decreased quality (Rich and Erb, 2005).

Illinois has been relatively slow to adopt managed care in its public health care programs and was among the last states to apply for and implement Medicaid waivers that would allow it to experiment with managed care arrangements. While some states moved rapidly to introduce managed care as a cost containment tool, shifting nearly 100% of their Medicaid beneficiaries into managed care arrangements, Illinois has been more hesitant, starting later, making it voluntary, and still having only about 10% of its Medicaid population in managed care.

Managed Care in Illinois
Enrollment Figures for the Illinois Medicaid Managed Care Program

As of October 2004, total enrollment in the voluntary managed care program in Illinois' Medicaid program was 170,862 participants. Of the total enrollment, 149,886 participants (87.7%) were enrolled with an HMO while 20,976 (12.3%) were enrolled with the Managed Care Community Network. (CMS, Medicaid Managed Care, 2005). Illinois was ranked with only four other states that had Medicaid managed care enrollment percentages below 10%. In fact, Illinois (9.13%) has the fifth lowest enrollment of all the States including the Virgin Islands, Puerto Rico and the District of Columbia. As of June 30, 2004, only Alaska (0%), New Hampshire (7.89%), South Carolina (6.47%), Virgin Islands (0%), and Wyoming (0%) had fewer of their Medicaid enrollees in Managed Care arrangements (Ibid). Illinois lagged far behind the national average, with only 9.13% of its Medicaid beneficiaries enrolled in one of five managed care companies in the state in 2004. All but one of these managed care companies operated exclusively in Cook County. The other also operated in the East St. Louis area, but none operated in any other area of the state (CMS, Medicaid Managed Care Plan Level Data by State, 2004).

Illinois' slow uptake of managed care may have been due to the national controversy surrounding some of the management techniques employed by managed care organizations. During the second half of the

1990s, a "backlash" against managed care developed in which consumers and providers claimed that managed care had not reduced costs or increased efficiency (Goldman et al., 1995; and Sullivan 2000), had led to patient dissatisfaction (Blendon et al., 1998; Gawande et al., 1998; and Simon, 1999), and its management techniques had resulted in adverse medical outcomes (Schulman, Sheriff and Momany 1997; Pegram, 2000[3]).

Despite this backlash, many of the features of managed care should be attractive to Illinois' Medicaid administrators, including its abi lity to negotiate price discounts with physicians and hospitals (Altman, Cutler, and Zeckhauser, 2000: 4), reduce the use of the most costly tests (Miller and Luft, 1995) and expensive technology (Cutler and Sheiner 1997: 5-6), shift the location of care from more costly inpatient care to less expensive outpatient settings (Gottlieb and Einhorn, 1997), and ensure that only medically necessary care is delivered.

ERISA and Managed Care Court Cases from Illinois

Illinois has been the source of two major Supreme Court cases in the last five years that have helped to frame the national debate over managed care. Both of these cases relate to one of the most important pieces of legislation governing American health care policy: the Employee Retirement Income Security Act (ERISA). In these two cases, Illinois became the stage for the national debate, and these two landmark decisions now represent accepted legal precedent for discussions of the relationship between corporate managed care organizations, patients, and state health care regulators.

The two cases from Illinois dealt with different issues and they had substantially different outcomes. The first was fully supportive of managed care organizations, freeing them from legal liability for the eligibility decisions they make. The second placed more restrictions on MCOs, allowing states to require external review of those eligibility decisions.

In its unanimous decision in the 2000 case *Pegram v. Herdrich,*[4] the Supreme Court dealt with whether the financial incentives placed on providers by the managed care organization adversely affected their treatment decisions. In upholding the basic tenets of managed care organizations' financial arrangements with providers, the Court reasoned that rationing health care is integral to all HMOs and that drawing a line between good and bad HMOs is best left to the legislative process. The Court found no reason for ERISA to supplant state malpractice law, which the plaintiff could still rely on to pursue her claim against the treating physician.[93]

In the 2002 case *Rush Prudential HMO v. Moran*,[5] the Supreme Court, in a 5 to 4 decision, found that states could require external review of unfavorable utilization review decisions made by HMOs, because this requirement is legitimately part of state insurance regulation.[6] Because an HMO is both a health care provider and an insurer, the Court found that state law does apply.[7]

Prescription Drugs

In 2003, $163 billion was paid for retail prescription drugs in the US, and this represented an 8.3% increase from 2002. Prescription drugs are the fastest growing component of health care costs, which is a consequence of changing demographics of the population, as well as increased reliance on prescription medications in medical therapy. There has been an increase in both the number of people taking prescription medications and the number of prescriptions per capita. As a proportion of total national expenditures, prescription drugs accounted for 9.4% in 2000, and are projected to increase to 12.9% by 2007 (Heffler et al., 2002: 208).

These rising costs have also prompted some state leaders to propose drug discount programs or importation of prescription drugs from other countries. Texas and Minnesota are among nine states, including Illinois, to begin discussions about drug importation and who provide information about Canadian pharmacies on their official state websites (Konig, 2005). Other recent state actions have included implementing prior authorization requirements, preferred drug lists, lower payments for drug products, co-payments, and limits on the number of prescriptions per month (Kaiser Family Foundation, 2005). According to a recent Kaiser Family Foundation survey of state Medicaid agencies, Illinois expects to have to narrow pharmacy benefits for its general Medicaid population in 2006. Furthermore, many state governors believe that Medicaid overpays for prescription drugs, and President Bush's current budget proposal would set a federal ceiling on prices paid for drugs, based on the average wholesale price (AWP) (National Governors' Association, 2005).

Prescription Drugs in Illinois

Illinois ranked sixth in the nation for personal expenditures for prescription drugs, with $6.8 billion spent by state residents in 2003. This actually represented a decrease of 0.6% from the 2002 expenditure figures. In 2002, Illinois spent $340 million for prescription drugs for state employees and retirees, and $1.8 billion for all state health programs combined (Office of the Governor, Letter to Tommy Thompson, December 22, 2003).

In 2004, Illinois' Medicaid program paid $1.28 billion for prescription drugs, which represented almost 20% of total Medicaid expenditures, and the second highest category of spending behind inpatient hospitals services (Kaiser Family Foundation, 2005). Because of Medicaid's role in covering low-income Medicare beneficiaries, also known as "dual-eligibles," Illinois expects increases in prescription drug costs to be a major cost driver for the Medicaid program in fiscal year 2006. In 2003, Illinois covered 190,102 "dual-eligibles," paying out almost $582 million for prescription drug coverage for this group.

Illinois has used the Medicaid 1115 Demonstrations waiver option to address one aspect of its prescription drug problem. Flexibility under section 1115 is sufficiently broad to allow states to test substantially new ideas of policy merit. In 2002, Illinois received approval for a pharmacy waiver for its program "Prescription Drug Benefit for Illinois' Low -Income Seniors." (CMS press release, January 28, 2002). The plan would allow the state to extend prescription drug coverage to almost 370,000 low-income seniors. It expands the previous state-funded plan, known as the "Circuit Breaker" program, which only provided coverage for chronic and catastrophic drugs. The new program includes limited cost-sharing applied on a sliding scale based on beneficiaries' income. It also offers a rebate to help pay for private insurance premiums for those beneficiaries who already have private insurance pharmacy benefits.

Governor Rod Blagojevich placed Illinois at the forefront of the national debate over prescription drugs costs in 2004 when he announced a plan to join a handful of other states in importing less expensive drugs from Canada, Ireland, and the United Kingdom. The Governor's office expects the I-SaveRx program will be able to provide savings of between 25% and 50% compared with prescription drugs purchased at American pharmacies. Wisconsin, Missouri, Kansas, and Vermont have also joined the program (Office of the Governor, Welcome to I-SaveRx, 2005).

Medical Malpractice Reform

There is a growing debate across the country over what many are calling a medical malpractice "crisis." The American Medical Association (AMA) has described 20 states, including Illinois, as being in crisis because of rising medical liability insurance premiums, and several states have developed legislation designed to address the issue (AMA, June 14, 2004). In 2004, New Jersey, Connecticut, Kentucky, and Nevada all introduced reform proposals ranging from reducing the amount of liability coverage physicians are required to carry to creating independent review of malpractice claims prior to going to trial to imposing caps on damage awards resulting from malpractice claims. In 2005, three states[8] reported reduced malpractice insurance premiums and influxes of new physicians after caps on non-economic damages were introduced the year before (Norbut, 2005).

Despite this experience in a few states, recent research in this area suggests that caps on damage awards may not solve the problem of increasing malpractice insurance premiums for physicians because the recent increase in malpractice premiums are not related to the amount of malpractice awards, but to underlying insurance cycles (Black, et al., 2005). Nonetheless, caps on non-economic damage awards are among the strategies currently being proposed in many state legislatures, including Illinois.

Malpractice in Illinois

In 2000, a total of $271 million was awarded to malpractice

plaintiffs in Illinois, and, according to the Illinois State Medical Society (ISMS), 92% of that was awarded for non-economic damages. The average medical malpractice payment made by physicians in Illinois in 2003 was $499,197 (Department of Health and Human Services, 2003).

Medical malpractice reform is among the highest priorities for the ISMS, which claims that doctors are leaving the state or refusing to perform certain procedures in order to avoid liability. ISMS has also pushed for legislation that would create malpractice caps on pain and suffering awards, and restrict the types of cases that can be brought in the state. Data from the Illinois State Medical Society suggest that between 1997 and 2002 in Illinois, the average total jury verdict increased by 61% and the average jury award for non-economic damages increased by 132% (ISMS, 2004). Recent ISMS reports also show that more than 30 malpractice insurers have gone bankrupt or left this state in the past five years, and that Illinois physicians are leaving some jurisdictions, especially in Madison and St. Clair Counties in the St. Louis area (Stanek, 2004).

Madison County in the East Metro area of St. Louis is considered a national hotbed of medical malpractice litigation. In fact, several cases have been moved there by plaintiffs' attorneys who have "shopped" for friendly jurisdiction in which to argue their cases. This is because Madison County is notorious for having the highest rate of malpractice verdicts favorable to the plaintiff of all jurisdictions in the country.

In 2004, Illinois State Senator Kirk Dillard introduced legislation that would place caps on damage awards in malpractice cases as well as creating other restrictions on malpractice plaintiffs and their lawyers. ISMS and the Heartland Institute believe that such caps would reduce the rate of malpractice insurance premiums for providers in Illinois and increase access to care for patients, but this stance is controversial. Senator Dillard's proposed bill, the Medical Liability Crisis and Access to Care Law of 2004, would have expanded good-faith immunity for health care professionals who provide emergent or volunteer care, prohibit multiple extensions on filing certificates of merit, and increase qualifications for expert witnesses to require that they be board-certified or board-eligible in the same specialty as the defendant (Dillard, 2004).

The essential controversy is not whether increases in medical malpractice premiums is a problem for providers in Illinois, but what solutions are likely to fix the problem. Caps on damage awards, as ISMS is advocating, may reduce the burden on some physicians and encourage them to stay in the state, but they are unlikely to solve the larger problem of increasing costs of medical malpractice, or of rising costs of health care overall.

The Future for Health Care in Illinois

As we noted at the beginning of this chapter, Illinois is a microcosm for the nation as a whole. This is certainly true in health care, where the state is in the midst of a major renegotiation of priorities and responsibilities in a variety of areas of health care policy. Current proposals are bold, and critics of some of the proposals have pointed out that many of the plans are untested and, perhaps, too costly or even unworkable.. Yet, successful new political alliances have been formed around the critical issue of access to quality health care for all Illinois residents. Tensions between increasing access and constraining costs will continue to dominate the health care reform debate in the state, and Illinois policymakers face a number of important choices in the months and years to come.

Questions about what strategies to emphasize to expand coverage under the Health Care Justice Act and how to pay for the projected costs of the All Kids program after the initial five year roll-out period are likely to frame the debates over these programs and in the health care policy arena more generally. Illinois policymakers will continue to be pressured to find strategies to reduce both state and personal expenditures on prescription drugs, especially as both costs and demand for drugs are projected to increase substantially throughout the next decade. .

Illinois will also be faced with the question of whether to continue to restrict the development of managed care or begin to embrace its potential for cost savings in the state's publicly financed health care programs. If the proposed shift to a primary care case management arrangement for low-income children and families in the state is any indication, it appears that

Illinois has crossed the threshold into the era of managed care, albeit a modified form from the one that transformed the health care system in this country during the 1990s.

The eyes of the nation will be on Illinois with the implementation of the All Kids program. Citizens and policymakers alike will be interested in the success of this program and in the performance of the health care system in terms of providing affordable, high-quality health care services.

References

Altman, Daniel, David Cutler, & R. J. Zeckhauser, *Enrollee Mix, Treatment Intensity, and Cost in Competing Indemnity and HMO Plans*, NATIONAL BUREAU OF ECONOMIC RESEARCH, Working Paper No. 7832, (August 2000) at http://nber.org/papers/w7832

American Medical Association, Massachusetts Becomes 20th State in a Medical Liability Crisis, Press Release, June 14, 2004, available at: http://www.ama-assn.org/ama/pub/category/13964.html

Appleby, Julie, States Take Health Care Problem in Own Hands: 19 Consider Insurance Fixes, *USA Today*, Nov. 8, 2005, p. 5B.

Aquilar, Alexa, Governor Blagojevich will offer plan for uninsured, St. Louis Post-Dispatch, Wednesday, Oct. 5, 2005.

Black, Bernard S., Charles Silver, David A. Hyman, & William M. Sage, Stability, Not Crisis: Medical Malpractice Claim Outcomes in Texas, 1988-2002. *Journal of Empirical Legal Studies*, Vol. 2 No. 2, p. 207-259 (July 2005).

Blendon, Robert J., John T. Young, Marie C. McCormick, Martha Kropf & Johnny Blair, American's Views on Children's Health, *Journal of the American Medical Association* 280(24), 2122 (1998).

Center for Medicare and Medicaid Services, HHS Approves Illinois Plan To Expand Medicaid Prescription Drug Coverage To Low-Income Seniors: Administration's "Pharmacy Plus" Project To Help Other States Create Similar Programs, Press Release, Jan. 28, 2002, available at: http://www.hhs.gov/news/press/2002pres/20020128a.html

Center for Medicare and Medicaid Services, Illinois Title XXI Program and Amendment Fact Sheet, May 27 2004, available at: http://www.-

cms.hhs.gov/schip/factsheets/chpfsil.pdf

Center for Medicare and Medicaid Services, Medicaid at a Glance, 2003, available at: http://www.cms.hhs.gov/states/maaghm.asp

Center for Medicare and Medicaid Services, Medicaid Managed Care Plan Level Data by State, June 30, 2004, available at: http://www.cms.-hhs.gov/medicaid/managedcare/er04net.pdf

Cutler, David & Louise Sheiner, *Managed Care and the Growth of Medical Expenditures*, National Bureau of Economic Research, Working Paper No. 6140, (August 1997) at http://papers.nber.org/papers/w6140.pdf

Dillard, Kirk, Medical Liability Crisis and Access to Care Act of 2004, Health Care News, The Heartland Institute, April 1, 2004, available at: http://www.heartland.org/Article.cfm?artId=14635

Fronstin, Paul, Sources of Health Insurance and Characteristics of the Uninsured: Analysis of the March 2004 Current Population Survey, Employee Benefits Research Institute, Issue Brief, No. 276, Dec. 2004.

Gawande, Atul A., Robert Blendon, Mollyann Brodie, J. M. Benson, L. Levitt & L. Hugick, "Does Dissatisfaction with Health Plans stem from having no Choices?" *Health Affairs* 17(5), 184 (1998).

Goldman, Dana P., Susan D. Hosek, Lloyd S. Dixon & Elizabeth M. Sloss, The Effects of Benefit Design and Managed Care on Health Care Costs, *Journal of Health Economics* 14(401) (1995).

Gottlieb, Scott & Thomas A. Einhorn, Managed Care: Form, Function, and Evolution, *Journal of Bone & Joint Surgery* 79(1), 125 (1997).

Heffler, Steven, Sheila Smith, Greg Won, M. Kent Clemens, Sean Keehan, & Mark Zezza, Health Spending Projections for 2001-2001: The Latest Outlook, *Health Affairs* 21(2) 207-218 (2002).

Holahan, John & Lee Nichols, "State Health Policy in the 1990's," in Robert F. Rich and William D. White, eds., *Health Policy, Federalism, and the American States 1996*.

Illinois Hospital Association, State to Borrow $1 Billion to Address Medicaid Payment Backlog, Oct. 17, 2005, available at: http://www.ihatoday.org/-issues/payment/medicaid/pymtbacklog.htm

Illinois State Medical Society, The Case for Malpractice Reform in Illinois,

Health Care News, The Heartland Institute, April 1, 2004, available at: http://www.heartland.org/Article.cfm?artId=14634

Kaiser Family Foundation, State Health Facts: Medicaid and SCHIP, FY2004 available at: http://www.statehealthfacts.org/cgi-bin/healthfacts.cgi?action=-compare&welcome=1&category=Medicaid+%26+SCHIP (last visited Nov. 15, 2005).

Kaiser Commission on Medicaid and the Uninsured, Access to Care for the Uninsured: An Update, Kaiser Family Foundation, Sept. 2003, available at: http://www.kff.org/uninsured/upload/Access-to-Care-for-the-Unin-sured-An-Update.pdf

Kaiser Commission on Medicaid and the Uninsured, Medicaid Budgets, Spending, and Policy Initiatives in State Fiscal Years 2005 and 2006, Oct. 2005, available at: http://www.kff.org/medicaid/upload/Medicaid-Budgets-Spending-and-Policy-Initiatives-in-State-Fiscal-Years-2005-and-2006-report.pdf)

Konig, Susan, Texas Postpones Drug Importation from Canada, Health Care News, The Heartland Institute, Oct. 1, 2005, available at: http://www.-heart-land.org/Article.cfm?artId=17760

Managed Care National Statistics, National Managed Care Enrollment 2004, Managed Care Fact Sheets, 2005, available at: http://www.mcareol.-com/factshts/factnati.htm

Miller, Robert H. & Harold S. Luft, Estimating Health Expenditure Growth Under Managed Competition: Science, Simulations, and Scenarios, *Journal of the American Medical Association* 273(8), 656 (1995).

National Association of State Budget Officers, *The Fiscal Survey of States*, June 2005, Washington, D.C., available at: http://www.nasbo.org/-Publications/-fiscalsurvey/fsspring2005.pdf

National Governors'Association, Medicaid Reform: A Preliminary Report, June 15, 2005, available at: http://www.nga.org/Files/pdf/0506-medicaid.pdf

Norbut, Michael, *Three Crisis' States Show Improvement after Tort Reform*, The Heartland Institute, May 1, 2005, available at:

http://www.heartland.-org/Article.cfm?artId=16859

Office of the Governor, Letter to Tommy Thompson, Dec. 22, 2003, available at: http://www.affordabledrugs.il.gov/letterhhs.cfm

Office of the Governor, Governor Blagojevich poised to make Illinois only state in the nation to offer comprehensive health coverage to every child All Kids plan wins final legislative approval; Governor to sign legislation. Oct. 27, 2005, available at: http://www.illinois.gov/-PressReleases/ShowPress-Release.cfm?SubjectID=1&RecNum=4416

Office of the Governor, Governor Blagojevich signs landmark legislation to provide comprehensive health coverage for every uninsured child in Illinois, Nov. 15, 2005, available at: http://www.illinois.gov/Press-Releases/ShowPressRelease.cfm?SubjectID=1&RecNum=4463

Office of the Governor, Welcome to I-SaveRx, 2005, available at: http://www.i-saverx.net/

Parnell, Steve, Vt. Governor Vetoes Single-Payer Plan, Health Care News, The Heartland Institute, August 1, 2005, available at: http://www.heartland.-org/Article.cfm?artId=17495

Parsons, Christi & Judith Graham. October 23, 2005. All Kids Proposal Stirs New Skeptics: Financial future may be shaky. *Chicago Tribune.* http://www.chicagotribune.com/features/health/chi-0510230544oct23-,1,7253692.story

Rich, Robert F. & Christopher T. Erb, The Two Faces of Managed Care Regulation & Policy Making. *The Stanford Law and Policy Review*, 16(1), 233-276 (2005).

Rosenbaum, Sara, Alexandra Stewart, & Colleen Sonosky, Negotiating the New Health System: Findings from a Nationwide Study of Medicaid Primary Care Case Management Contracts. Center for Health Care Strategies, Working Paper MCBP227-402, June 2002.

Rosenbaum, Sara & Brian Kamoie, Managed Care and Public Health: Conflict and Collaboration, *Journal of Law, Medicine & Ethics* 30(191) (2002).

Schulman, Elizabeth D., Jean Doris Sheriff & Elizabeth T. Momany, Primary Care Case Management and Birth Outcomes in the Iowa

Medicaid Program, *American Journal of Public Health* 87(1), 80 (1997).

Simon, Steven R., Views of Managed Care, *New England Journal of Medicine* 340(12), 928 (1999).

Stanek, Steve, Doctors Flee Illinois, The Heartland Institute, April 1, 2004, available at: http://www.heartland.org/Article.cfm?artId=14633

Sullivan, Kip, On the 'Efficiency' of Managed Care Plans, *Health Affairs* 19(4), 139 (2000).

US Department of Health and Human Services, National Practitioner Data Bank, 2003 Annual Report, available at: http://www.npdb-hipdb.com/-pubs/stats/2003_NPDB_Annual_Report.pdf

Weissert, Carol S. & William G. Weissert, *Governing Health: The Politics of Health Policy, 1996.*

Notes

[1] There are a variety of waiver programs available to states wishing to experiment with innovate arrangements for Medicaid, including Section 1115(a), 1915(b), and HIFA waivers. For example, Section 1915 waivers permit states to enroll beneficiaries in managed care plans and to provide home and community based services. Community based services were initiated in the 1980s for the elderly and people with disabilities to reduce institutional care and costs. Waivers under Section 1115(a) of the Social Security Act allow states to provide services through the vehicle of Research and Demonstration Health Care Reform Program. Under this waiver program, states can expand managed care to include HMOs, partially capitated systems, primary care case managers, or other variations.

[2] A description of the HIFA waiver program and states'experiences with it are available online at: http://cms.hhs.gov/hifa/default.asp

[3] *Pegram v. Herdrich* was a 2000 Supreme Court case examining the question of whether managed care organizations can be held liable for adverse health outcomes resulting from medical treatment decisions by physicians within their provider networks. See our discussion of this case as it pertains to Illinois' experience with managed care in the following section of this chapter.

[4] *Pegram v. Herdrich,* 530 U.S. 211 (2000).

[5] *Rush Prudential HMO, Inc. v. Moran,* 536 U.S. 355 (2002).

[6] *Id.* at 373; *See generally,* E. Haavi Morreim, *ERISA Takes a Drubbing: Rush Prudential and its Implications for Health Care*, 38 TORT & INS. LAW J. 3, 933-961(2003) (showing that 42 states and the District of Columbia have provisions for independent review of medical necessity determinations and discussing their implications for the future of ERISA preemption).

[7] *Rush* 536 U.S., at 367.

[8] Ohio, Texas, West Virginia.

Chapter 4

Long-Term Care Reform in Illinois

Naoko Muramatsu

The state plays a critical role in long-term care (LTC) policy, financing, and delivery in the United States. The federal Medicare program does not cover LTC except for limited home health nursing and skilled nursing services. Medicaid, the federal-state program for the poor, on the other hand, covers the greatest share of public LTC services, including nursing home and home and community-based services (HCBS). Given minimum standards set by the federal government, states are the agents for LTC reforms.

As in other states, the long-term care system in Illinois faces a number of challenges: the system of services is heavily biased toward nursing homes as opposed to the home and community settings; financing and delivery of services are fragmented and not very responsive to people's needs; and elders face limited access to needed services. Seniors and advocates are demanding changes to our LTC system; the state budget faces unprecedented shortfalls and at the same time, legislators and state department leadership are beginning to acknowledge the need for reform. The growing advocacy network calling for LTC reform and bipartisan legislative support led to the passage of SB2880, signed by the Governor in August 2004, followed by his signing of HB5057, which called for reintegration of more able nursing home residents into the community. This series of events and intensive activities have produced a broad consensus that LTC in Illinois needs to be transformed.

Following up this momentum, the University of Illinois Institute of Government and Public Affairs (IGPA), together with the Health and Medicine Policy Research Group (HMPRG), convened a one-day conference, entitled *"Long Term Care in Illinois: The Next Generation."* The goal of this conference was to assemble key Illinois stakeholders to learn from other states where substantial reform efforts are under way or have been put in place and to discuss specific short-term and long-term LTC reform options. The conference's capstone were working groups of Illinois providers and advocates who had the task of integrating what they had heard into priorities for this state. This chapter highlights key LTC issues in Illinois, summarizes the important findings and outcomes of this conference, describes the ongoing LTC reform efforts in Illinois subsequent to this conference, and discusses future directions for LTC policy and research.

Why Is Long-Term Care an Important Public Policy Issue in Illinois?

Most seniors want to spend the last stage of life at home (Flory et al., 2004). However, LTC services are mainly provided in the institutional setting. Home and community-based services (HCBS), including personal assistance and transportation, are to provide alternative LTC to allow seniors to stay in the home and the community. It has been recognized the importance of rebalancing the LTC system from the one centered on nursing homes to the one with appropriate access to HCBS (Kane, Kane, and Ladd, 1998). States are making progress in this regard, partly driven by the Olmstead Decision by the Supreme Court of 1999, which mandates states to provide community-based services for persons with disabilities who would otherwise be entitled to institutional services. Historically, states vary greatly in their efforts and commitment to rebalance the LTC. Illinois has made progress in increasing per-capita HCBS expenditures and the share of LTC expenditures spent on HCBS, but Illinois still lags behind other states in shifting LTC from a nursing home centered system to a more balanced one with appropriate access to HCBS. In 2002, Illinois ranked 40th in HCBS expenditures per person 65 and over and 35th in the proportion of LTC expenditures spent on HCBS among 50 states and the District of Columbia (Muramatsu and Hoyem, 2004). To rebalance the LTC system in Illinois, institutional LTC resources should be shifted to HCBS programs. Illinois has the fifth highest nursing home bed capacity per person 65 and older in the country, but it has the eighth lowest nursing home occupancy rates

(Muramatsu and Hoyem, 2004). However, significant reallocations in LTC resources have been difficult in Illinois partly because of a politically powerful nursing home industry.

Illinois faces other important LTC issues. For example, LTC programs have developed around various funding sources (e.g., Medicaid, state general revenues, allocated Older American Acts moneys, Social Service Block Grants), resulting in administrative complexity and services gaps. Medicaid is the largest funding source of LTC in Illinois as in any other state. Funding for HCBS in Illinois characterized by a large amount of the state's general revenues support for HCBS, most of which is spent on the Community Care Program (CCP) that provides in-home and adult day services to people 60 or over whose "countable" assets are $12,500 or lower. CCP is unique in that it is an entitlement program because of the court order (*Benson v. Blaser*). A major problem of services that have evolved around various constituencies related to various programs is that, while seniors and people with disabilities are likely to need a number of acute and long-term care services concurrently, available services are not well-coordinated to meet such needs. Furthermore, the current public programs are mainly for the poor, with Medicaid as the leading financial source, while the majority of Americans are not protected against potentially catastrophic costs of long-term care. The private LTC insurance market is growing steadily but its impact is limited, partly because of its prohibiting costs for consumers. Also, benefits covered by many private LTC insurance policies are limited. Many Americans are not aware of their vulnerability against long-term care needs.

Long-Term Care in Illinois: The Next Generation

To advance discussion and move long-term care reform in Illinois toward more substantial systems change, the IGPA conference engaged the stakeholders essential for reforming the LTC system in Illinois (legislators, agency administrators, agency staff, advocates, researchers, public health workers, older adults and family members, disability advocates, and health care associations).[1]

We envisioned this event to be a learning and working conference at which participants could jointly develop short-term and long-term visions and specific plans for LTC reform in Illinois. Thus, our major goals were to involve all the major stakeholders in Illinois, learn from other states where long-term care reform is well under way, translate the lessons from other states into the context of Illinois, and contribute to a substantive system reform. We believe that we have achieved the major goals mentioned above, evidenced by the substantial and serious exchanges among the participants and by the list of participants that included two Illinois legislators, all the directors of the four state agencies critical for long-term care systems reform, and the heads of the major organizations related to LTC.

Summary of Important Findings and Outcomes

States will continue to be the engine for long-term care reform. Other states, faced with a number of common challenges in financing, delivery, quality, and workforce issues, have developed a number of innovative programs and means for organizing and delivering services. States vary in terms of their vision, strategies, focus, political processes, and scope of their reforms, while all of them struggle with common issues, such as turf issues between agencies and Medicaid. A few themes for effective reforms emerged: consolidation (streamlining regulations and putting the authority for such programs under one agency and one budget), the executive branch's initiatives, the importance of having a vision to function as an anchor that would transcend changes in state administration, financial situations, and leadership. Other states'experiences indicated the importance of the timing (taking advantage when windows of opportunity arose), focusing on what was possible, paying attention to the process, and setting specific bench marks.

Illinois now has a window of opportunity for significant LTC reform. With leaders who have vision and a commitment to reform at the key state agencies and in the legislature, some specific initiatives and efforts have already begun. Examples include expansion of eligibility criteria for the state's home and community -based services under the Illinois Department on Aging, and nursing home quality improvement under the Illinois Department of Public Health. State agencies have started regular ongoing dialogues, and a coalition of advocates and stakeholders led to the passage of SB2880 and HB5057.

Several specific themes emerged from the panel of Illinois legislators and agency leaders:

- reverse our thinking and require a waiver to place a person in a nursing home rather than helping them remain in the community;
- develop a vision;
- secure real resources to back up reforms;
- create a seamless system that entitled the person to a range of services no matter his or her age;
- educate the public about LTC issues;
- seek the executive branch's leadership and active involvement;
- commit to living wages for long-term care workforce;
- create incentives to make nursing homes right-sized;
- improve the regulatory process;
- make the system responsive to people's needs rather than financing.

The panelists differed in their opinion about resources required for reforms. While some advocated for securing resources to meet the needs through raising state income taxes, taxing retirement income, and modernizing the sales tax, others advocated for more in-kind contribution of resources through community-based efforts. They also noted the problems that Illinois will continue to face, such as trying to engage the executive branch, competing demands for funding within the Medicaid program, turf issues across agencies, and the power of the nursing home industry (which, as one the literature notes, is a problem that most states face).

Priority areas for LTC reform in Illinois, as identified in the sessions, included:

o develop a knowledgeable, broad-based constituency for LTC reform through a major educational and grassroots coalition building effort;

o develop a high quality workforce with living wages and career ladder opportunities;

o shift resources away from facility based to home and community based services through approaches such as demonstration projects, a special legislation, a new omnibus waiver, or a county tax;

o redesign the delivery system (e.g., expand CCP, create a single or coordinated point of entry, implement "money follows the person"[2]);

o develop more adequate responses to caregiver needs;

o explore integrating aging and disability services/ stakeholders.

The conference provided a powerful impetus to the efforts now under way to change the LTC system in Illinois. A keynote speech by Josh Wiener, a Senior Fellow at RTI International, provided a well-developed context in which state reform efforts could be situated. Direct exchanges with the leaders of successful reform efforts in other states helped Illinois stakeholders to collectively learn about other states' successful legislative and administrative strategies, pitfalls to avoid, organizing tactics used, evaluation of the results to date, and alternatives available in Illinois contexts. This conference also provided the basis for developing infrastructure changes that are necessary for more systematic LTC reforms in Illinois: development of strong cadre of legislators, researchers and other constituencies; comprehensive e-mail and mailing lists to organize people into working groups after the conference; and involvement of university researchers from multiple disciplines who can bring knowledge bases and skills into the LTC reform process as needed.

The Older Adult Services Act and Ongoing
Long-Term Care Reform Activities in Illinois[3]

With the passage of SB2880 as mentioned above, the Older Adult Services Act (P.A. 0993-1031) was implemented in 2004, which supports seniors to stay in their homes by restructuring the delivery of services to include home and community-based services as well as institutional services. This law requires the expansion of services to older adults and their family caregivers, subject to availability of funds, and development of rules to implement the law and an annual report of progress. It designates the Illinois Department of Aging (IDOA) as the lead agency and calls for collaboration between IDOA, Department of Public Health (IDPH), and Department of Healthcare and Family Services (formerly Department of Public Aid). This law also calls for the development of a Nursing Home Conversion Program to be established by the state departments of Public Health and Healthcare and Family Services. The program would reduce reliance on nursing homes by Medicaid. Savings from this effort would be re-allocated to a broader array of options for home-based or community-based services to older adults. According to the Act, the IDOA designated a 32-member Advisory Committee, which consists of representatives from a variety of statewide associations, senior service organization representatives, citizen members, and family caregivers. This committee meets at least quarterly to advise the directors of the Departments of Aging, Public Health, and Healthcare and Family services on various initiatives required by the Act. In addition, as of October 2004, five work committees have been established to address issues related to workforce and caregiver, nursing home conversion, services, point of entry, and finance.

Future Directions

Illinois has started serious efforts to reform long-term care. In order to turn this momentum into a system change, it is essential to continue to build coalition among consumers, providers, researchers as well as state legislators and agency leaders, learn from "best practices" from other states, and develop plans that are best suited for Illinois.

Research plays a critical role in LTC policies and reform efforts (Kemper, 2003). It is important to analyze state policies that are directly and indirectly related to LTC, assess possible policy changes, and evaluate their impact on consumers and various stakeholders.

Despite the salient role in the states in U.S. LTC policies, little is known about how state LTC policies, especially levels of commitment to HCBS, affect individual older persons' trajectories of LTC use and well being (Muramatsu and Campbell, 2002). In order to fill this gap, the author is currently conducting research, with funding from the National Institute on Aging, to investigate how trajectories of LTC utilization and well-being among older Americans vary over time as a function of state LTC policies. Our findings indicate that those who live in states more generous in HCBS services have a lower risk of entering a nursing home and the effects of a state's gen erosity in HCBS on the risk of nursing home admission were more salient among those with fewer family resources. Also, our research to date suggests that greater resources devoted to community-based care at the state level may reduce likelihood of death in a nursing home or while a resident of a nursing home. It is important to monitor the trend of state commitment to HCBS and other state LTC policy and service contexts so that we can continue to examine their effects on key outcomes among older Americans and people with disabilities.

While states will continue to be the agents for LTC reforms for the foreseeable future, it is also important to pay attention to how national policy changes impact the range of reforms to be done at the state level. So far, the United States has managed LTC piecemeal, relying on the welfare system and private payment. Other countries, such as Germany and Japan, have adopted an alternative approach to assure access to LTC for their residents, regardless of socioeconomic status (Tsutsui and Muramatsu, 2005). Many tasks remain before any consensus on even broad goals on LTC policies can be reached in the United States. However, developing and assessing various policy alternatives is a critical step toward future LTC reforms both at the national and state levels.

References

Flory, J., Y. X. Yinong, et al. 2004. Place of Death: U.S. Trends Since 1980. *Health Affairs* 23(3): 194-200.

Kane, R.A., R.L. Kane, and R.C. Ladd. 1998. *The Heart of Long Term Care.* New York: Oxford University Press.

Kemper, P.. 2003. Long-term care research and policy. *The Gerontologist, 43*(4):436-446.

Muramatsu, N. and R.T. Campbell. 2002. State Expenditures on Home and Community Based Services and Use of Formal and Informal Personal Assistance: A Multilevel Analysis. *Journal of Health and Social Behavior, 43*(March). 107-124.

Muramatsu, N. and R. L.Hoyem. Funding Streams for Long Term Care: Trends in Illinois. Background paper for Long Term Care in Illinois: The Next Generation, September 14, 2004, Chicago Illinois. http://www.igpa.uiuc.edu/health/pdf/Muramatsu__Hoyem.pdf and http://www.hmprg.org/pdf/Muramatsu%20&%20Hoyem.pdf.

Tsutsui, T. and N. Muramatsu. 2005. Care Needs Certification in the Long-Term Care Insurance System of Japan. *Journal of American Geriatrics Society, 53*:522-527.

Notes

[1]More information about the conference is available at http://www.igpa.-uiuc.edu/news/pressReleases/sept04.htm; http://www.igpa.uiuc.edu/health/, and http://www.hmprg.org/pdf/jvg_ltc.pdf.

[2] The term "money follows the person" refers to "a system of flexible financing for long-term services that enables available funds to move with the individual to the most appropriate and preferred setting as the individual's needs and preferences change." This definition and more detailed information is available in a report by Crisp S. et al., *Money Follows the Person and Balancing Long-Term Care Systems: State Examples* at the Center for Medicare and Medicaid Services website: http://new.cms.hhs.gov/PromisingPractices/Downloads/mfp92903.pdf

[3] More information about the Older Adult Services Act and its related activities are available at the IDOA website (http://www.state.il.us/aging/1athome/-oasa/oasa.htm).

Chapter 5

Public Financing of Mental Health and Developmental Disability Services[1]

Lorens A. Helmchen

The public financing of services for persons with developmental disabilities or mental illness is part of the state's social insurance commitment to shield these population groups from the risk of financial hardship that disabilities of this kind entail. As such, the state pays providers to serve patients, and the provider reimbursement system plays an important role in achieving the goals of a social insurance system that provides residential, therapeutic, and rehabilitation support for persons with developmental disabilities and mental illness.

Any reimbursement system should strive to be transparent and affordable. It should be transparent in that it makes explicit the eligibility criteria for receipt of services, the standard of care, and the desired level of patients' health and well -being. It should be affordable in that it attains these goals at minimum cost to the taxpayer.

Notably, both the level and the structure of the provider reimbursement system will affect the ability of the program to achieve its goals.

In this regard, the existing method of reimbursing providers by specifying separate payment rates for a large number of inputs is deficient on several dimensions. Most importantly, the overall level of expenditure for serving persons with developmental disabilities or mental illness is unlikely to be the least-cost expenditure because the state does not know what the true costs are and it is too costly to obtain this information in a timely manner. Thus, the state will set reimbursement rates incorrectly and too many generously reimbursed services will be provided and not enough poorly reimbursed services will be provided. Not only will such reimbursement affect the cost of providing care, but it will also distort providers' choice of inputs and the quality of care delivered.

In addition, as providers are paid for inputs, they may overuse or overreport their use of resources and thus inflate the cost of service provision without a corresponding guarantee that specified outcomes are achieved. By limiting the quantity of services allowed, the state attempts to counteract the tendency of beneficiaries to overutilize services. Presumably, however, the optimal volume of services varies across individuals; therefore, while a uniform cap may be simpler to implement, it may allow some persons to overconsume, while forcing others to underconsume.

For most services, the desired treatment outcome is never really specified beyond noting that services should be provided according to a person's needs. Yet, without explicit target levels of patients' health and well-being, society at large, and developmentally disabled and mentally ill persons and their stakeholders in particular, cannot know which level of quality and access the state is aiming to attain for them and how well the current reimbursement system is succeeding in achieving this goal.

In the following, alternative reimbursement mechanisms are presented that hold the promise of allowing the state to purchase a given level of quality at lower cost; make the state's expenditure on services for persons with developmental disabilities or mental illness more predictable; give patients and their stakeholders greater ability to choose the kind of service they prefer; and encourage providers to innovate and reduce cost.

Define a Standard of Quality to Achieve
Transparency and Accountability

The current reimbursement system relies heavily on paying providers to use specific inputs in specific proportions to provide care. Yet, this neither guarantees that specific levels of patient health and well-being are achieved, nor does it guarantee that the cost of achieving these health and well-being standards is minimized.

Therefore, the state should consider developing a set of indicators that reliably measure all aspects of the beneficiary's health and well-being that are affected by the provider's quality of service. The adoption of such a set of quality indicators and the choice of their associated target values effectively defines an explicit standard of quality. In this way, the state reveals the level of care that it is committed to achieving for its citizens who suffer from developmental disabilities or mental illness. An explicit definition also constrains the state in its ability to gradually renege on this commitment. In other words, defining an explicit minimum standard of patient health and well-being makes the goals of the state, and of society in general, transparent; and it allows patients to hold the state accountable if these goals are not attained. Consequently, instead of reimbursing providers for the inputs they use, the state should reimburse providers for achieving carefully defined levels of health and well-being among the patients in their care.

Create an Auditing and Penalty Mechanism to Minimize Abuse

If quality is costly to provide, providers may be tempted to reduce quality. Yet, mentally ill and developmentally disabled persons often cannot assess the quality of services they receive or cannot articulate complaints about quality. As a result, they are at risk of being subject to abuse by providers. To minimize this risk, reliable systems to monitor outcomes must be put in place by the state.

Some quality indicators are less costly to obtain than others. Therefore, to remain credible, the state's choice of quality indicators will be limited by the resources it will devote to auditing providers.

The audit mechanism can consist of two components:

o An independent contractor that carries out recurring but unpredictable spot checks.
o A grievance process, by which patients and their stakeholders can alert the independent contractor about providers whose service is alleged to be substandard.

To complement its audit mechanism, the state should penalize providers who fail to adhere to the standards they contract to achieve. This penalty could consist of revoking the provider's right to compete for service provision in the future; it could also involve monetary fines or prison sentences.

Use Prospective Payments to Encourage Innovation in Service Provision

Once a standard of quality has been defined, providers should be paid to achieve this level and given maximum flexibility in attaining that standard. This is best achieved through a prospective payment system. This mechanism encourages innovation and cost control because it leaves providers free to choose or develop the technology and combination of inputs that are most efficient. However, to reduce risk selection whereby providers avoid high-risk program participants, some part of provider payment should be based on retrospective costs. For example, providers can be made responsible for the first 10% of any expenditure that exceeds the contracted payment. Beyond this expenditure, providers may receive additional payments.

Use Competition Among Providers to Maximize Cost Efficiency

As outlined above, prospective payment systems obviate the need for providers to report cost, but they also make the state liable to overpay for services. To encourage providers to pass on their cost savings to the state, all providers that satisfy the minimum standard of quality should have to compete to serve patients. As they compete for patients, the technologically most efficient providers will be able to offer the best quality at the lowest price and thereby attract additional patients. At the same time, less efficient providers will lose patients. In this way, competition among providers and choice by patients or their guardians will ensure that the state's expenditures are continuously shifted to the most efficient providers. As a result, the state avoids overpaying for services.

Two mechanisms that have providers compete for serving Illinois citizens who suffer from developmental disabilities or mental illness can be distinguished: competition for contracts and competition for enrollees. Under the first, providers compete for a contract to serve all members of a well-defined population; under the second, providers compete for serving members of this population individually.

Competition for Contracts

Under this award mechanism, the state defines the population to be served and also sets the minimum level of care that providers must offer recipients. Providers compete for contracts to provide, at the specified level of quality, services to all persons in a defined geographic area who meet the eligibility criteria established by the state. The provider offering to serve this population at the lowest price is awarded the contract. In practice, the state could request that providers submit their contract terms on a specific date and then select the best offer or it could keep accepting successively better offers from additional providers within a certain time frame. For example, the state could publish how much it is paying current awardees and periodically invite new providers to compete for these contracts.

In this type of competition, the most efficient provider will win the contract and typically will make a profit. The prospect of earning a profit encourages potential providers to enter the competition, thereby putting pressure on current awardees to innovate. This process ensures that providers'efforts to reduce cost continue to translate into lower expenditures by the state.

Profits also deter current providers from cheating on the contract: Only if it is profitable to serve persons who suffer from developmental disabilities or mental illness, providers will find it costly to lose this business. In particular, if the penalty for noncompliance is the lost profit, any increase in profit that providers could achieve by noncompliance would raise the penalty for doing so by the same amount. In this way, providers'fear of losing this profit will promote greater compliance than a fixed penalty payment set by the state. Specifically, if the penalty amount is set too low, providers may find it cheaper to cheat and pay the fine than to comply.

Under this system, there are two ways in which incumbent providers can lose the contract:

o They are found to be providing care below the contracted level of quality, in which case the contract is terminated and the provider may be excluded from participating in future rounds of competition.

o They are undercut by a lower-cost competitor's offe r at the next, periodically held round of competition.

These two reasons for possible discontinuation of a provider's contract suggest that the state has two levers to raise the likelihood of compliance.

o More frequent auditing of quality raises the probability that a noncompliant provider will lose his profit and thereby raises the expected penalty payment.

o Less frequent rounds of competition raise the period of time that providers who were awarded a contract will be protected from lower-cost competitors. The longer intervals between rounds of competition raise providers' profits and thereby the penalty payment if they are found to violate the terms of the contract.

If incumbent providers anticipate that they will lose their contract in the next round of competition, however, future profits will decline, as the contract period draws to an end. In this case, the prospect of losing future profits in case of noncompliance will not provide enough of an incentive to maintain quality toward the end of the contract period. Therefore, it may be optimal to gradually add a fine that increases as the end of the contract draws nearer, so that the penalty for noncompliance matches the provider's entire profits throughout the contract period.

This award mechanism encourages a maximum of innovation and cost control because providers are free to choose or develop the technology and combination of inputs that reduce cost most while maintaining the mandated level of care. As providers compete for contracts, their competitive offers to win the contract will reflect their true cost of serving the defined population at the mandated level of care, thereby passing on any cost advantages to the state.

On the other hand, given that providers aim to minimize expenditure, they may cut quality in those dimensions that are hardest to measure and audit by the state. Thus, competition for contracts will fail to take into account those patient preferences that are both costly to satisfy and costly to monitor objectively. The state will have to decide whether any additional expenditures to audit providers' compliance with these, mostly intangible, dimensions of care are justified by the additional health and well-being of the program beneficiaries.

Once eligibility is defined, the risk of variation in the actual number of patients claiming care is borne by the providers, so that once the contract has been awarded, the state's expenditures for providing services are perfectly predictable for the duration of the contract.

In addition, the fact that one organization is in charge of providing services to the entire population of patients defined by the state prevents providers from serving only the most profitable segments of this group, such as patients whose needs of medical attention and overall supervision are minimal or who can work for pay in a suitably adapted environment.

At the same time, however, the state is liable to define the population covered in each contract in a way that does not allow providers to deliver services at minimum cost. For instance, a larger patient population may enable a given provider to spread fixed costs such as on-the-job training of staff, construction of care facilities, program administration, or negotiations with suppliers over a greater number of beneficiaries and thereby reduce expenditure per capita. In this case, the state would forego these cost savings if it chose too small a beneficiary population to be included in the contract.

To implement this award mechanism, the state needs to set up an effective auditing system of quality control to ensure that providers actually deliver on the quality they committed to when they were awarded the contract. For instance, patients and their guardians should be informed about the quality that the state has purchased for them and that they are entitled to receive. As outlined above, an easily accessible grievance process that allows patients or their guardians to report a breach of contract would help alert the state about noncompliance. In addition, third-party licensure bodies can be used to examine all provider organizations that want to participate in the competition and to enforce minimum standards of care among the contract awardees.

The state also needs to prevent current and prospective providers from conspiring to submit worse offers when they compete for contracts than if they acted independently. This is achieved best if the eligibility criteria to participate in the competition are transparent. Also, the more profitable the contract for potential providers, the more firms will enter the contest, and the harder it will become for contestants to coordinate the terms of their offers.

Competition for Enrollees

Instead of defining a minimum level of care and having providers compete to serve a specific population at the lowest cost, the state can set a fixed payment amount and let providers compete on the basis of quality of service. To ensure that enough providers will find it attractive to compete, the state can gradually raise the payment until the number and variety of competitors promise to guarantee a predetermined minimum level of care.

Once the pool of qualified providers has been defined, the state grants vouchers to all eligible recipients of services. Each program beneficiary, in conjunction with family members and his or her guardian, then selects a provider who accepts the voucher in lieu of payment. Note that this award mechanism would allow relatives or friends to care for the patient and to be compensated at the same rate as institutional providers.

Competition for program beneficiaries among providers will ensure that recipients receive the highest quality of care that is technologically feasible at the set payment level. At the same time, the state no longer chooses a provider for the recipient. As in the case of competition for contracts, this system maximizes providers' flexibility in delivering care and rewards those who innovate and cut cost. In particular, under this mechanism, the state does not specify the size of the patient population served by a provider. Instead, providers are allowed to vary in size. For example, urban providers may take advantage of centrally located day-care facilities and serve a larger number of patients than rural providers, for whom the cost of transporting the patient between the home and the day-care setting or workplace may be more important.

In contrast to competition for contracts, providers have a strong incentive to exceed the minimum standard of care by satisfying those intangible patient preferences that are cheap to honor but very costly to monitor objectively. As the provider choice now rests with patients instead of the state, the variety of services offered will match the diversity of patients much more closely than under competition for contracts. For instance, providers may try to fill market niches by choosing to build group homes close to relatives, specialize in treating a subset of patients who suffer from a specific developmental disability or mental illness, or offer differentiated menus of day-care activities and meals that cater to distinct patient groups.

By allowing patients to "detect and defect," the state enlists the help of the users themselves to broaden the range of quality variables that are monitored. Compared to the model of competition for contracts, this mechanism of selecting providers imposes greater demands on recipients' ability to evaluate the services they receive and to exercise their option of switching providers effectively. Periodic review of facilities and certification of personnel by the state can ensure that patients, regardless of their choice of provider, receive a minimum level of care. In addition, active involvement of guardians, family relatives, and other stakeholders in patients' welfare can help recipients choose the provider that is best for them.

The state's expenditure per beneficiary is predictable under this system, but the state bears any risk of unforeseen fluctuation in the number of beneficiaries.

In contrast to competition for contracts, which forces awardees to serve all members of a well-defined patient population, providers competing for enrollees might design services in such a way that attracts low-cost patients and deters high-cost patients. In this way, providers would be able to serve only the most profitable beneficiaries, leaving the most costly patients without care. To prevent this form of risk selection, it would be necessary to offer additional reimbursement to providers who care for the most difficult patients. For example, beneficiaries'v ouchers might vary in size according to fixed and observable characteristics that reliably predict the cost of treating the patient. Similarly, providers might be granted additional compensation if they demonstrably incurred above-average cost to treat the most severe cases.

As in the case of competition for contracts, the state must prevent providers from conspiring to lower the level of care for all beneficiaries, which would render useless patients' option to "detect and defect ." Transparent rules of certification to participate in the competition for enrollees and an effective appeals system for providers who feel they are denied the right to compete minimize the cost to potential providers of participating in the competition. At the same time, the higher the payment that providers can expect for serving the mentally ill and developmentally disabled, the more potential providers will find it profitable to serve this population, resulting in more vigorous competition.

These recommendations would increase the ability of the state to provide mentally ill or developmentally disabled persons with a quality of services that is both transparent and affordable. They would strengthen the confidence of patients, providers, and the public that tax revenues dedicated to serving this population are spent effectively and fairly.

Note

[1] I would like to thank Robert Kaestner for valuable discussions throughout the preparation of this article.

Chapter 6

Children's Health Care in Illinois:
Where are We and Where are We Going?

Robert F. Rich and Cinthia L. Elkins

The health of American children has improved over recent generations, yet the quality of children's health continues to represent a critical public policy issue nationally and in Illinois. Up to three-quarters of children do not receive recommended health care to prevent disease, reduce disease complications, and achieve optimal health and development. Twenty-three percent of the children in the state of Illinois live in poverty, which is the average for the nation.[1] Health disparities exist with poor and minority children more likely to receive inadequate care; their level of care varies substantially across geographic regions. These variations cannot be accounted for in terms of differential health care needs.

States are uniquely positioned to make significant improvements in the quality of health care for young children, due to their roles as administrators of Medicaid and the State Children's Health Insurance Program.[2] This chapter will outline the state of children's health in Illinois and depict how it compares to other states in the area of child health, child health insurance, and access to health care for children. It will also describe the current plans of the state for making improvements in these areas.

If one examines "children's health status ," we find that Illinois falls very close to the national average on a number of health status measures. Health disparities exist for Illinois children as they do for children in the rest of the nation. This can be illustrated by looking at some of the findings from the "National Survey of Children's Health ." These data show that 90.8% of white Illinois parents report that their children's heath is "excellent" or "very

70

good"; however, this was true for only 64.5% of Hispanic parents 79.3% of African-American parents, 86.4% of multiracial parents, and 70.1% of "others."[3] In 2002-03, 81% of Illinois children ages 19 to 35 months were immunized[4], slightly higher than the national average of 78%. However, 86% of white children were immunized while only 79% of Hispanic children were fully immunized.[5]

In 2000, an estimated 37.2% of births in Illinois were financed by Medicaid.[6] Illinois ranked 20th of states in rates of prenatal care; 84.9% of women get prenatal care, which puts the state very close to the national average of 83.7% of women receiving prenatal care. However, in 2002, the percent of Illinois mothers beginning prenatal care in the first trimester was 90.8% of white women but only 74.2% of African American women and 78.4% of Hispanic women. This shows a larger disparity than the national averages of 88.6% of white women, 75.2% of African American women, and 76.7% of Hispanic women.[7] In Illinois in 2003, 11.1% of births to white women, 18.4% of births to African American women, and 11.6% of births to Hispanic women were pre-term. This is slightly higher than the national average for all three ethnic categories.[8]

Access is also an important component of any health care system. Insurance coverage is one measure of access.[9] Illinois is about average in this area, as well. In 2003-04, 63% of children in Illinois had employer-sponsored/private health insurance, 5% had individual/private health insurance, 20% had Medicaid, 1% had other public insurance, and 11% were uninsured.[10] These data follow the national average fairly closely.[11] Of Illinois children who live under the Federal Poverty Level (FPL), 17% had employer insurance, 4% had individual insurance, 52% had Medicaid, and 26% were uninsured in 2003-04. Relative to the national average, Illinois has a slightly higher number of uninsured children and a slightly lower number of Medicaid-covered children.[12]

It is also worth noting that in recent years, Illinois has been making changes and advances in providing health insurance to children. Before the State Children's Health Insurance Program was created by Congress in 1997, Illinois had not developed a child health insurance program separate from the benefits provided as part of Medicaid. In late 1998, before the KidCare program began in Illinois, there were an estimated 212,297 children living in families with incomes below 250% of the Federal Poverty Level and without health insurance. Cook County (Region IV) had the highest percentage of uninsured children at 23.69%. The more rural regions of the state (Regions I, II, and III) had lower percentages of uninsured children, at 16.27%, 13.08%, and 11.13%, respectively.[13]

KidCare represents the Illinois version of the State Children's Health Insurance Program (SCHIP), which is a federally funded block grant program. This initiative provides states with substantially more policy-making and administrative authority than they ever possessed in previous intergovernmental health care programs.[14] "KidCare" is administered by the Illinois Department of Healthcare and Family services (formally the Department. of Public Aid), and was approved by the Center for Medicare and Medicaid Services, in April 1998. Illinois pays 35 percent of the total costs of their SCHIP program (the federal matching rate is 65 percent) and has a capped allotment of federal funds each year (the federal fiscal year 2004 allotment to Illinois was $120,969,643).

The program started as an expansion of Medicaid, making more children eligible for the same benefits. Then, in November of 1998, an amendment was submitted to add a separate child health insurance program, administered separately, and with a set of benefits different from those provided by Medicaid. This expanded coverage to children less than 19 years of age with family incomes between 133% and 185% of the Federal Poverty Level (FPL). KidCare includes five different insurance plans based on income level. (See appendix for a description of these plans). In June of 2003, Illinois expanded coverage for children enrolled in KidCare by raising the upper income eligibility limit from 185% of the FPL to 200% of the FPL. The latest amendment on February 23, 2004, implemented "presumptive eligibility" for children during the period after an application has been submitted but prior to the determination of eligibility.[15] This allows children to receive health-care services while their application is being fully processed.

A national study of State Children's Health Insurance Programs has found that while this form of health insurance is a source of coverage for millions of children, it has also introduced new inequities in access to insurance. SCHIP is imperfectly targeting eligible children who are uninsured, and it's financing is "problematic" because of the block -grant funding structure and use of SCHIP funds to cover adults.[16] How does Illinois SCHIP, KidCare, compare to other states?

When examined in the context of the performance of other states, Illinois has been doing comparatively well in some areas. In December 2004, Illinois ranked 8th of the states in SCHIP enrollment, with 122,711 children enrolled that month.[17] In 2003, Illinois ranked 40th of all state programs with 18% of their eligible children enrolled in KidCare. In 2004, Illinois rose to 18th with 36% of eligible children ever enrolled. That was the second largest percent improvement (73% increase) of all states; going from 135,609 ever enrolled in 2003 to 234,027 ever enrolled in 2004.[18] The Kaiser Commission on Medicaid and the Uninsured similarly showed with point-in-time enrollment data[19] Illinois has been a national leader in expanding access to health care for children and families. Illinois was second in the nation in the second half of 2003 in the number of children added to the States Children's Health Insurance Program (KidCare). In addition, the Kaiser commission reported that Illinois was first in the nation in adding parents to its SCHIP program, increasing enrollment of parents by 227 percent.[20]

Illinois has been one of the leaders in expanding and improving children's health insurance programs. The Illinois Department of Public Aid (now Health and Family Services) stepped up its outreach efforts in 2004 by partnering with local school systems and by working more closely with its network of more than 1,100 KidCare application agents around the state along with private sector partners, such as Jewel-Osco, to promote the KidCare program.[21].

In July 2003, Governor Blagojevich signed legislation that expanded the eligibility level for children under SCHIP from 185 percent to 200 percent of the Federal Poverty Level (FPL and expanded Family Care eligibility for parents from 49 percent to 90 percent of the FPL. In 2004, the

Family Care eligibility was further expanded to 133 percent of the FPL, pushing the income level for coverage from $16,968 to $25,068 for a family of four. In addition, as already noted, enrollment has been made easier and faster by adopting "presumptive eligibility, [22] and by requiring only 1 pay-stub for income verification

The state employs various measures to encourage eligible children to enroll, utilize, and stay in the program. These measures include media campaigns involving radio, print and promotional advertising; establishing educational partnerships, especially with the Chicago Public Schools, to assist in promoting public awareness and assist with enrollment; and establishing strong community outreach through employers, churches and other community- based organizations. In addition to the above outreach efforts, the Department contracts with KidCare Application Agents statewide to perform the following functions:

○ Collaborate with other community groups such as schools, social services agencies, and churches to promote KidCare.
○ Identify families with children who are likely to be eligible for KidCare.
○ Assist families to complete applications, including assembling required documentation.
○ Submit completed applications for determination of eligibility.

The State reimburses the KidCare Agents a $50 Technical Assistance Payment for each complete KidCare application submitted that results in enrollment in KidCare. [23]

Although this is a very positive program, there are some areas where the outcomes have fallen short of the objectives. Based on 2003 Census data, 253,000 children in Illinois are still without health insurance. More than half of them come from working and middle class families who earn 'too much' to qualify for programs like KidCare, but cannot afford private health insurance.[24]

Many families who are enrolled in Medicaid or SCHIP still do not have access because of geographic location. Illinois has 846 health professional shortage areas, and, even in non-rural parts of Illinois, the low-income population is nationally recognized as "health professional shortage" populations. Health Professional Shortage Areas (HPSAs) have shortages of primary medical care, dental or mental health providers and may be geographic (a county or service area), demographic (low-income population) or institutional (comprehensive health center, federally qualified health center or other public facility).[25]

In addition, Illinois is already more than $1 billion behind in its payments to Medicaid providers with some doctors waiting months for payment.[26] The current payment delay to health care providers who treat Medicaid patients is 66 days.[27] Many doctors and hospitals are not accepting new Medicaid/KidCare patients because they are not fully reimbursed for their costs by the state and the state has fallen behind in paying its bills. In addition, Medicaid reimbursement rates are among the lowest in the country. On average, in 2003, hospitals were paid at 71% of the cost of providing care to Medicaid beneficiaries.[28] As a result, hospitals are threatening to or are actually dropping out of the program, refusing to see Medicaid patients. This affects Children on the lowest level of KidCare (assist) because it is an expansion of the Medicaid program.

The state has authorized a $1 billion short-term loan (which must be repaid by the end of the fiscal year), which will garner $1 billion in matching federal funds. It will reduce the current payment delay to health care providers who treat Medicaid patients from 66 days to less than 30 days, according to Michael Moss of the Illinois Department of Healthcare and Family Services. However, that payment cycle will again lengthen to the 75 days set during the 2004 budget negotiations.[29]

These financial difficulties are due to a number of factors. Cost of prescription drugs and rising health care costs in general are a major challenge for Illinois as they are for every other state. Also, Illinois is among the states with the lowest Federal Medicaid Assistance Percentage (FMAP) at 50%: an increase in federal matching percentage could help Illinois expand coverage and benefits.[30]

One cost-saving strategy used by most states' Medicaid programs that Illinois has not taken full advantage of is managed care. By October 2004, Illinois had enrolled only 170,862 of its total 1,580,000 eligible Medicaid beneficiaries in managed care plans (11%), and it contracted with five different managed care entities to provide health care services. This enrollment figure represents an 18.6% increase in managed care over 2003, but was still one of the lowest in the country (the average was 59%). Less than 10% of Illinois' Medicaid funds are expended in managed care arrangements. As of December of 2004, Illinois ranked 47th of the states in the percentage of state Medicaid enrollees in Medicaid Managed Care.[31]

In response to some of these issues, Illinois has undertaken a revision of its state children's health insurance program. In late October of 2005, the Illinois state legislature approved the Covering ALL KIDS Health Insurance Act. This program plans to make comprehensive health insurance available to all children, with parents paying monthly premiums and co-payments for doctor's visits and prescription drugs at rates based on their income level. All Kids would also offer access to hospital stays, vision care, dental care, and medical devices like eyeglasses and inhalers.[32] It would make Illinois the first state to offer comprehensive coverage to all uninsured children. It is the Governors' intent to have this program implemented by July of 2006.[33]

The All Kids program would offer Illinois' uninsured children comprehensive health care that includes doctor's visits, hospital stays, prescription drugs, vision care, dental care, and medical devices like eyeglasses and asthma inhalers. Parents will pay monthly premiums for the coverage, but rates for middle-income families will be significantly lower than they are on the private market. For instance, a family of four that earns between $40,000 and $59,000 a year will pay a $40 monthly premium per child, and $10 co-pay per physician visit. However, there will be no co-pays for preventive care visits, such as annual immunizations and regular check-ups and screenings for vision, hearing, appropriate development, or preventative dental care. The state will cover the difference between what parents contribute in monthly premiums and the actual cost of providing health care for each child, expected to be $45 million in the first year. [34]

In order to finance this new program, Governor Blagojevich proposes shifting the state's 1.7 million Medicaid patients into managed health care, a cost-savings move with which other states have substantial experience. At a time when most people with private insurance are in some type of managed care, all but a few Illinois patients in state-subsidized health care are not. State public aid officials estimate that the change to a system called "primary care case management" (PCCM) would save $57 million next year, more than enough to cover the $45 million they think it would cost to expand health-care coverage for uninsured children during the same period. Under this system, most Medicaid members in Illinois would be assigned a doctor who would oversee their care for a small monthly fee, in addition to customary fees for each service they provide. By contrast, in an HMO system, doctors typically are paid only a flat monthly sum. The plan would ensure that every family has their own family physician and would save money. The experience of other states shows that this system does contain costs. This occurred because Medicaid members were assigned to primary doctors, got more routine care, and were hospitalized less often.[35] The theory is that by insuring for preventative care "early-on", fewer people will need expensive specialized care or emergency are for critical conditions.

As with any new and ambitious governmental program, there are skeptics and critics with concerns about the viability of the plan. The main concern voiced is financial sustainability. Because Illinois is already more than $1 billion behind in its payments to Medicaid providers with some doctors waiting months for payment, critics are questioning the viability of the proposal. Some experts consider the PCCM model to be a 'throwback', a 'looser, ki ndler, gentler managed care model," that has been replaced by more rigorous managed care models in urban areas.[36] However, twenty-nine other states have realized significant savings by using this model for their Medicaid programs. Based on independent analysis, the Department of Healthcare and Family Services estimates that Illinois will save $56 million in the first year by implementing the PCCM model in all state health programs except for those that serve the elderly and the blind.[37] Other experts argue that this new plan "doesn't in any way address the long -term sustainability of Medicaid. The fundamental problem is that Medicaid is taking up an increasingly large share of the state budget." [38] The chief "architects" of All Kids predict that after five year s, the cost of the plan would be financed by the savings that are produced. Up to this point in time, the economic forecasts do not extend beyond the five-year mark. [39]

Conclusion

Overall, in the area of children's health care, the State of Illinois is doing slightly better than the nation as a whole with recent outstanding improvements and great promise for the future. Despite a downturn in the economy and recent state budget cuts, children's health has remained a high priority for Illinois. Steady expansions of state health insurance programs and expanding eligibility have assured that the numbers of uninsured children have been steadily dropping even while the number of uninsured adults is growing due to employers dropping their health insurance programs. Steps have been taken to continue to improve the children's health insurance program despite fiscal problems in Illinois and for the nation as a whole.

The new All Kids program holds promise and is another step in the direction of improving access of children to health insurance. The success of this new program will depend on a sound fiscal plan, the viability of the PCCM model of care, and its ability to work with providers so that they are able to participate without financial duress. In addition, the problem of physician and health professional shortage areas needs to be addressed to assure that children can access health care and to guarantee for the viability of the insurance coverage. However, with the implementation of this program, Illinois may be well on its way to becoming a leader in children's health care.

Appendix

KidCare includes five plans. Each program has varying eligibility and cost sharing requirements based on the FPL and financial responsibility:

- o KidCare Assist - Children with family income at or below 133% of the FPL enroll and receive services through the State's Medicaid Program under Title XIX or through the Phase I expansion under Title XXI. Premiums are not imposed for families at or below 150% of the FPL.
- o KidCare Moms and Babies - Pregnant women with family incomes at or below 200% of the FPL and their babies up to age one receive benefits with no cost-sharing requirements. This plan is under the State's Title XIX program.
- o KidCare Share - This plan provides benefits for children with family income between 133% and 150% of the FPL, who are not covered by KidCare Moms and Babies. No premiums, but a $2 co-payment for medical visits and prescriptions and non-emergency use of the emergency room. There is a $100 annual co-payment maximum for all families. This plan is under Title XXI.
- o KidCare Premium - KidCare Premium provides benefits for children with family income above 150% up to 185% of the FPL, who are not covered by KidCare Moms and Babies. Premiums are $15 per month, with two children $25 per month, and $30 per month for three or more children. There are also $5 co-payment for medical visits, a $3 co-payment for generic, and $5 co-payment for brand-name prescriptions and a $25 co-payment for non-emergency use of the emergency room. There is a $100 annual co-payment maximum for all families. This plan is under Title XXI.
- o KidCare Rebate - This plan is available to those whose children are insured and who have family incomes above 133% and up to 185% of the FPL. KidCare Rebate reimburses part of the cost for private health insurance for children.

Source: http://www.cms.hhs.gov/schip/factsheets/chpfsil.pdf

Table A1: Rank Order of Percent of Eligible Children Ever Enrolled in SCHIP, 2003

State	Eligible Children 2003	Ever Enrolled 2003	Percent Enrolled 2003
1. Maryland	182000	130161	71.52%
2. New York	1203000	795111	66.09%
3. Rhode Island	42000	24505	58.35%
4. Missouri	263000	150954	57.40%
5. Alaska	42000	22934	54.60%
6. Maine	59000	29474	49.96%
7. Florida	947000	443177	46.80%
8. Nebraska	98000	45490	46.42%
9. Georgia	546000	251711	46.10%
10. Kentucky	228000	94053	41.25%
11. Massachusetts	316000	128790	40.76%
12. Texas	1871000	726428	38.83%
13. Oklahoma	237000	91914	38.78%
14. South Carolina	238000	90764	38.14%
15. Colorado	209000	74144	35.48%
16. California	2812000	995152	35.39%
17. New Jersey	353000	119272	33.79%
18. North Carolina	463000	150444	32.49%
19. Nevada	147000	47183	32.10%
20. Mississippi	237000	75010	31.65%
21. South Dakota	39000	12288	31.51%
22. Ohio	672000	207854	30.93%
23. West Virginia	116000	35320	30.45%
24. Kansas	156000	45662	29.27%
25. Pennsylvania	573000	160015	27.93%
26. Virginia	307000	83716	27.27%
27. Louisiana	390000	104908	26.90%
28. Iowa	138000	37060	26.86%
29. Wisconsin	265000	68841	25.98%
30. Alabama	303000	78554	25.93%
31. Utah	152000	37766	24.85%
32. Indiana	321000	73762	22.98%
33. Delaware	46000	9903	21.53%

34. Oregon	224000	44752	19.98%
35. New Hampshire	50000	9893	19.79%
36. Arizona	466000	90468	19.41%
37. Vermont	35000	6467	18.48%
38. District of Colombia	32000	5875	18.36%
39. Illinois	742000	135609	18.28%
40. Montana	74000	13084	17.68%
41. Connecticut	126000	20971	16.64%
42. Idaho	106000	16877	15.92%
43. Wyoming	34000	5241	15.41%
44. Michigan	531000	77467	14.59%
45. Hawaii	97000	12022	12.39%
46. North Dakota	46000	4953	10.77%
47. New Mexico	195000	18841	9.66%
48. Washington	299000	9571	3.20%
49. Minnesota	203000	4366	2.15%
50. Arkansas	213000	.	0.00%
51. Tennessee	328000	.	0.00%

Table A2: Rank Order of SCHIP programs by Percentage of Children Ever Enrolled, 2004

State	# of Children 2004	Ever Enrolled 2004	% Covered 2004
1. New York	1130000	826611	73.15%
2. Missouri	250000	176014	70.41%
3. Massachusetts	279000	166508	59.68%
4. Rhode Island	43000	25573	59.47%
5. Maryland	192000	111488	58.07%
6. Alaska	38000	21966	57.81%
7. Maine	57000	28171	49.42%
8. Georgia	574000	280083	48.79%
9. Kentucky	232000	94500	40.73%
10. Florida	1054000	419707	39.82%
11. New Jersey	322000	127244	39.52%
12. Oklahoma	257000	100761	39.21%
13. Nebraska	85000	33314	39.19%
14. California	2701000	1035752	38.35%
15. South Dakota	36000	13397	37.21%
16. Ohio	602000	220190	36.58%
17. Mississippi	229000	82900	36.20%
18. Illinois	661000	234027	35.40%
19. North Carolina	511000	174434	34.14%
20. Texas	1937000	650856	33.60%
21. Iowa	125000	41636	33.31%
22. Pennsylvania	556000	177415	31.91%
23. West Virginia	116000	36906	31.82%
24. Virginia	314000	99569	31.71%
25. South Carolina	241000	75597	31.37%
26. Kansas	147000	44350	30.17%
27. Delaware	35000	10250	29.29%
28. Hawaii	66000	19237	29.15%
29. Wisconsin	248000	67893	27.38%
30. Utah	148000	38693	26.14%
31. New Hampshire	42000	10969	26.12%
32. Louisiana	407000	105580	25.94%
33. Nevada	149000	38519	25.85%
34. Indiana	317000	80698	25.46%

35. Alabama	314000	79407	25.29%
36. Vermont	27000	6693	24.79%
37. Colorado	241000	57244	23.75%
38. Montana	66000	15281	23.15%
39. Oregon	208000	46720	22.46%
40. Arizona	453000	87681	19.36%
41. District of Col	33000	6093	18.46%
42. Wyoming	30000	5525	18.42%
43. Idaho	106000	19054	17.98%
44. Michigan	488000	87563	17.94%
45. Connecticut	141000	21438	15.20%
46. North Dakota	35000	5137	14.68%
47. New Mexico	186000	20804	11.18%
48. Washington	306000	17002	5.56%
49. Minnesota	171000	4784	2.80%
50. Arkansas	215000	799	0.00%
51. Tennessee	320000	.	0.00%

Table A3: Rank of States by Percentage Change in SCHIP Enrollment, 2003 to 2004

State	Ever Enrolled 2003	Ever Enrolled 2004	% Change in Enrollment
1. Washington	9571	17002	77.64%
2. Illinois	135609	234027	72.57%
3. Massachusetts	128790	166508	29.29%
4. Virginia	83716	99569	18.94%
5. Montana	13084	15281	16.79%
6. Missouri	150954	176014	16.60%
7. Hawaii	16526	19237	16.40%
8. North Carolina	150444	174434	15.95%
9. Michigan	77467	87563	13.03%
10. Idaho	16877	19054	12.90%
11. Iowa	37060	41636	12.35%
12. Georgia	251711	280083	11.27%
13. New Hampshire	9893	10969	10.88%
14. Pennsylvania	160015	177415	10.87%
15. Mississippi	75010	82900	10.52%
16. New Mexico	18841	20804	10.42%
17. Oklahoma	91914	100761	9.63%
18. Minnesota	4366	4784	9.57%
19. Indiana	73762	80698	9.40%
20. South Dakota	12288	13397	9.03%
21. New Jersey	119272	127244	6.68%
22. Ohio	207854	220190	5.93%
23. Wyoming	5241	5525	5.42%
24. West Virginia	35320	36906	4.49%
25. Oregon	44752	46720	4.40%
26. Rhode Island	24505	25573	4.36%
27. California	995152	1035752	4.08%
28. District of Colombia	5875	6093	3.71%
29. North Dakota	4953	5137	3.71%
30. Delaware	9903	10250	3.50%
31. Utah	37766	38693	2.45%
32. Vermont	6541	6693	2.32%
33. Connecticut	20971	21438	2.23%

34. Alabama	78554	79407	1.09%
35. Louisiana	104908	105580	0.64%
36. Kentucky	94053	94500	0.48%
37. Maine	28474	28171	-1.06%
38. Wisconsin	68641	67893	-1.09%
39. Kansas	45662	44350	-2.87%
40. Arizona	90468	87681	-3.08%
41. Alaska	22934	21966	-4.22%
42. Florida	443177	419707	-5.30%
43. New York	896728	826611	-7.82%
44. Texas	726428	650856	-10.40%
45. Maryland	130161	111488	-14.35%
46. South Carolina	90764	75597	-16.71%
47. Nevada	47183	38519	-18.36%
48. Colorado	74144	57244	-22.79%
49. Nebraska	45490	33314	-26.77%
50. Arkansas	.	799	.
51. Tennessee	.	.	.

Notes

[1] Poverty exists when a family earns less than 100% of the Federal Poverty Rate. The federal poverty level for a family of three in the 48 contiguous states and D.C. was $14,680 in 2003 and $15,067 in 2004. Data from Urban Institute and Kaiser Commission on Medicaid and the Uninsured estimates based on the Census Bureau's March 2004 and 2005 Current Population Survey, available at: http://www.state-healthfacts.-kff.org/

[2] Smith, Vernon. *Issue Brief: The Role of States in Improving Health and Health Care for Young Children.* July 2005. Commonwealth Fund publication #843. www.cmwf.org/usr_doc/States_improving_hlt_young_children.pdf

[3] National Survey of Children's Health Data Re source Center, available at: http://nschdata.org/

[4] For the purpose of this data, immunized children are those who receive 4:3:1:3:3, which is four or more doses of diphtheria, tetanus, and pertussis, three or more doses of poliovirus vaccine, one or more doses of any measles containing vaccine (MCV), three or more doses of Haemophilius Influenza type B (Hib), and three or more doses of hepatitis B vaccine (HepB).

[5] *Estimated Vaccination Coverage with Individual Vaccines and Selected Vaccination Series Among Children 19-35 Months of Age by State -- U.S., National Immunization Survey, 2002-2003* National Immunization Program, Centers for Disease Control and Prevention, available at http://www.cdc.gov/nip/-coverage/NIS/02-03/toc-0203.htm .

[6] Maternal and Child Health (MCH) *Update 2002: State Health Insurance Coverage of Pregnant Women, Children, and Parents, National Governors Association*, Table 1, June 2003, available at http://www.nga.org/cda/files/-MCHUPDATE02.pdf.

[7] Martin JA, Hamilton BE, Sutton PD, Ventura SJ, Menacker F, Munson ML, Births: Final Data for 2002, National Vital Statistics Report, Vol. 52, No. 10, December 17, 2003, Division of Vital Statistics, National Center for Health Statistics, available at http://www.cdc.gov/nchs/data/nvsr/nvsr52/nvsr52_10.pdf

[8] Special Data Request, Division of Vital Statistics, National Center for Health Statistics, Centers for Disease Control and Prevention, 2003, available at http://www.statehealthfacts.kff.org/

[9] Other factors than insurance impact access to care, including transportation, number of doctors per population, ease of getting to and being seen by an available physician, etc. This is addressed more later in the chapter.

[10] Urban Institute and Kaiser Commission on Medicaid and the Uninsured estimates based on the Census Bureau's March 2004 and 2005 Current Population Survey (CPS: Annual Social and Economic Supplements), available at http://www.-state-healthfacts.kff.org

[11] National average is 56% employer-sponsored, 4% individual, 26% Medicaid, 1% other public, and 12% uninsured.

[12] Urban Institute and Kaiser Commission on Medicaid and the Uninsured estimates based on the Census Bureau's March 2004 and 2005 Current Population Survey (CPS: Annual Social and Economic Supplements), available at http://www.-statehealth-facts.kff.org

[13] McNamara, Paul E., Health Insurance Coverage in Rural Illinois. January 24, 2000. Presented at the Illinois Rural Health Association's Public Policy Workshop "Insuring the Health of Rural Illinoisans."

[14] Rich, Deye and Mazur, "The State Children's Health Insurance Program: An Administrative Experiment in Federalism." University of Illinois Law Review, Vol. 2004 No. 1.

[15] CMS Illinois State SCHIP Factsheets. Was available at http://www.cms.hhs.gov/schip/factsheets/chpfsil.pdf in November 2005. The fact sheet summary provides a overall sumary and history of the SCHIP state plan including all amendments.

[16] Kenney and Chang. September 2005. "The State Children's Health Insurance Program: Successes, Shortcomings, and Challenges." *Health Affairs* 23: No.5.

[17] States with larger programs were California, New York, Texas, Florida, Georgia, Ohio and Pennsylvania. Collected by Health Management Associates for the Kaiser Commission on Medicaid and the Uninsured. Data as of December 2004, published September 2005, available at http://www.statehealthfacts.kff.org

[18] Enrollment data from CMS annual enrollment reports http://www.cms.hhs.gov/NationalSCHIPPolicy/SCHIPER/itemdetail.asp?filterType=none&filterByDID=9&sortByDID=2&sortOrder=ascending&itemID=CMS032999. (Only Washington state is doing better with a 78% increase for having 9,571 enrolled in 2003 and 17,002 enrolled in 2004). See appendix for SCHIP enrollment tables.

[19] "Point-in-time" enrollment data looks that the number of children enrolled during a single month, while "ever-enrolled" numbers are all children who were enrolled at any point in time during the whole year.

[20] Governor announces KidCare tops enrollment target: Successful outreach campaign extends health Nov. 10, 2004 Press Release IGGN.coverage. Available at: http://www.illinois.gov/PressReleases/ShowPressRelease.cfm?SubjectID=6&RecNum=3519

[21] Governor announces KidCare tops enrollment target: Successful outreach campaign extends health Nov. 10, 2004 Press Release IGGN.coverage. Available at: http://www.illinois.gov/PressReleases/ShowPressRelease.cfm?SubjectID=6&RecNum=3519

[22] Governor announces KidCare tops enrollment target: Successful outreach campaign extends health Nov. 10, 2004 Press Release IGGN.

[23] CMS Illinois State SCHIP Factsheets. Was available at http://www.cms.hhs.gov/schip/factsheets/chpfsil.pdf in November 2005. The fact sheet summary provides a overall sumary and history of the SCHIP state plan including all amendments. However, when checked in January, 2006, the website is in flux and link is no good. Should be available at: http://www.cms.hhs.gov/LowCostHealthInsFamChild/04SCHIPStatePlanAndSummaryInformation.asp#TopOfPage now, but not yet functional. Tried to download files from http://www.cms.hhs.gov/LowCostHealthInsFamChild/SCHIPASPI/itemdetail.asp?filterType=none&filterByDID=-99&sortByDID=2&sortOrder=ascending&itemID=CMS028671but the link is incorrect and got Georgia instead of Illinois info.

[24] Governor Blagojevich's All Kids, Giving Every Child in Illinois Access to Good, Affordable Health Insurance, Powerpoint Presentation. Available at: http://www.allkidscovered.com/assets/111505_allkidspresentation.pdf .

[25] US Dept. of Health and Human Services, Health Resources and Services Administration, Bureau of Health Professions, Health Professional Shortage Area database, search performed in November 2005 (database continuously updated). Available at: http://hpsafind.hrsa.gov/HPSASearch.aspx.

[26] Parsons and Graham. October 23, 2005. All Kids Proposal Stirs New Skeptics: Financial future may be shaky. Chicago Tribune. Available for fee at online Chicago Tribune Archives: http://pqasb.pqarchiver.com/chicagotribune/access/915332131.html?dids=915332131:915332131-&FMT=ABS&FMTS=ABS:FT&type=current&date=Oct+23%2C+2005&author=Christi+Parsons+and+Judith+Graham%2C+Tribune+staff+reporters&pub=Chicago+Tribune&edition=&startpage=1&desc=All+Kids+proposal+stirs+new+skeptics+ .

[27] Massingale, Mary. Loan to Pay Medicaid a Quick fix: state backlog expected to continue to grow. Friday Nov. 4, 2005. Copley News Service. http://www.pjstar.com/stories/-110405/REG_B81G7PKM.049.shtml

[28] Illinois Hospital Association Medicaid Strategic Plan. September 2002. Available at: http://www.ihatoday.org/issues/payment/medicaid/-stratplan.pdf Approved by the IHA Board of Trustees: September 11, 2002 (projected SFY 2003 reimbursement data)

[29] Massingale, Mary. Loan to Pay Medicaid a Quick fix: state backlog expected to continue to grow. Friday Nov. 4, 2005. Copley News Service. http://www.pjstar.com/-stories/110405/REG_B81G7PKM.049.shtml

[30] Federal Register, June 17, 2003 (Vol. 68, No. 116), pp. 35889-35890, at http://a257.g.akamaitech.net/7/257/2422/14mar20010800/edocket.access.gpo.-gov/2003/pdf/03-15274.pdf. FY2005: Federal Register, December 3, 2003 (Vol. 68, No. 232), pp. 67676-67678, at http://aspe.os.dhhs.gov/health/fmap05.htm. FY2006: Federal Register, November 24, 2004 (Vol. 69, No. 226), pp. 68372. KCMU estimates of the multiplier are based on the FMAP.

[31] Medicaid Managed Care Enrollees as a Percent of State Medicaid Enrollees, as of December 31, 2004. Available http://www.statehealthfacts.kff.org/cgi-bin/healthfacts.cgi?-action=compare&category=Medicaid+%26+SCHIP&subcategory=Medicaid+Managed+Care&-topic=MC+Enrollment+as+a+%25+of+Medicaid+Enrollment .

[32] Office of the Governor, News Release, November 15, 2005 *Governor Blagojevich signs landmark legislation to provide comprehensive health coverage for every uninsured child in Illinois.* Available at: http://www.illinois.gov/PressReleases/ShowPressRelease.cfm?SubjectID=1&RecNum=4463

[33] State of Illinois, All Kids website. Available at: http://www.allkidscovered.com/ .

[34] Office of the Governor, News Release, November 15, 2005 *Governor Blagojevich signs landmark legislation to provide comprehensive health coverage for every uninsured child in Illinois.* Available at: http://www.illinois.gov/PressReleases/ShowPressRelease.cfm?SubjectID=1&RecNum=4463 .

[35] Parsons and Graham. October 23, 2005.All Kids Proposal Stirs New Skeptics: Financial future may be shaky. Chicago Tribune. Available for fee at online Chicago Tribune Archives: http://pqasb.pqarchiver.com/chicagotribune/access/915332131.html?dids=-915332131:915332131&FMT=ABS&FMTS=ABS:FT&type=current&date=Oct+23%2C+2005-&author=Christi+Parsons+and+Judith+Graham%2C+Tribune+staff+reporters&pub=Chicago+-Tribune&edition=&startpage=1&desc=All+Kids+proposal+stirs+new+skeptics+ .

[36] Parsons and Graham. October 23, 2005. All Kids Proposal Stirs New Skeptics: Financial future may be shaky. Chicago Tribune. Available for fee at online Chicago Tribune Archives: http://pqasb.pqarchiver.com/chicagotribune/access/915332131.html?dids=-915332131:915332131&FMT=ABS&FMTS=ABS:FT&type=current&date=Oct+23%2C+2005&-author=Christi+Parsons+and+Judith+Graham%2C+Tribune+staff+reporters&pub=Chicago+-Tribune&edition=&startpage=1&desc=All+Kids+proposal+stirs+new+skeptics+ .

[37] Office of the Governor, News Release, November 15, 2005 *Governor Blagojevich signs landmark legislation to provide comprehensive health coverage for every uninsured child in Illinois.* Available at: http://www.illinois.gov/PressReleases/ShowPressRelease.cfm?Subject-ID=1&RecNum=4463 .

[38] Parsons and Graham. October 23, 2005. All Kids Proposal Stirs New Skeptics: Financial future may be shaky. Chicago Tribune. Available for fee at online Chicago Tribune Archives:
http://pqasb.pqarchiver.com/chicagotribune/access/915332131.html?dids=915332131:915332131-&FMT=ABS&FMTS=ABS:FT&type=current&date=Oct+23%2C+2005&author=Christi+Parsons-+and+Judith+Graham%2C+Tribune+staff+reporters&pub=Chicago+Tribune&edition=&startpage=-1&desc=All+Kids+proposal+stirs+new+skeptics

[39] Parsons and Graham. October 23, 2005. All Kids Proposal Stirs New Skeptics: Financial future may be shaky. Chicago Tribune. Available for fee at online Chicago Tribune Archives: Available at http://pqasb.pqarchiver.com/chicagotribune/access/915332131.html?dids=-915332131:915332131&FMT=ABS&FMTS=ABS:FT&type=current&date=Oct+23%2C+2005&-author=Christi+Parsons+and+Judith+Graham%2C+Tribune+staff+reporters&pub=Chicago+-Tribune&edition=&startpage=1&desc=All+Kids+proposal+stirs+new+skeptics

Chapter 7

*Is There a Shortage of Child Care in Illinois?**

Rachel A. Gordon and Elizabeth T. Powers

Do most parents rely on family, friends, and neighbors to watch their children because of problems with access and affordability (there aren't enough child care centers in their community or the available slots are too expensive)? Or do these parents simply prefer that their children's early care experiences take place in a home setting?

Such questions underlie many current policy debates, proposals, and initiatives around child care in Illinois. Here, as in many other states, the majority of families who use subsidies pay for in-home rather than center-based care.[1] (See Box 1 for more on the types and cost of care). This heavy use of in-home care raises concerns for some because, although such settings may provide an optimal environment for some children, on average they offer fewer of the developmental inputs that have been linked to school readiness.

Recent needs assessments have called attention to this debate. Needs assessments attempt to enumerate and contrast the number of children in need of care with the number of child care slots in an area. The findings from these needs assessments have been used to argue that some families face extremely limited child care options, and that policies to directly increase the supply of licensed child care slots are the best response. In an influential 1999 study, the Illinois Facilities Fund identified apparent severe shortages in Chicago. In five communities, there were practically no full-day center care slots relative to the child population (Illinois Facilities Fund, 1999).

In this chapter, we enter the ongoing dialogue on child care shortages and public policy. We argue that needs assessments are just one

Box 1: Types and Costs of Child Care

Child care providers can be classified in a variety of ways. One clear distinction is between care that occurs in private homes and care that occurs elsewhere. Another clear distinction is between licensed and license-exempt care.

Care outside of private homes typically takes place in dedicated child care facilities called child care *centers*. Center-based care is organized around groups of same-age children. Under Illinois licensing standards, up to twelve infants may be cared for in a single group with a ratio of staff to children of no less than 1 to 4. Among three-year-olds, the group may contain up to twenty children with a staff to child ratio of 1 to 10 (DCFS, 2004b). In Chicago and its surrounding counties, the cost of full-time center-based care for infants averages $200 per week and the cost of full-time center-based care for three-year-olds averages $136 per week. In the least populous counties of the state, full-time care for infants averages $115 per week and for three-year-olds averages $87 per week. These amounts translate to between $4,000 and $10,000 per year for 50 weeks of care (author calculations based on Table 6 of DHS, 2003).

Early childhood education programs are sometimes classified together with child care centers. Many such programs, including those that fall under the auspices of the State Board of Education and enroll children who are at least three years of age, are exempt from DCFS licensing standards (DCFS, 2004a). These generally are preschool programs. Three important types of preschool programs that serve low-income children in Illinois are Head Start, the Illinois State Board of Education Pre-kindergarten at Risk Program, and the Chicago Parent-Child Centers. Typically, these programs differ from licensed child care centers in being part-day, part-year programs and in requiring higher educational credentials of staff, although increasingly collaborative models combine child care with preschool to offer full-day, full-year care (Chicago Partners for Children, 2003).

Home-based care takes place in a private home and may be licensed (often called *family day care*) or license-exempt (often called *family, friend and neighbor* care). In Illinois, home-based providers who care for more than three children (including their own) are required to be licensed (DCFS, 2004a). Most home-based providers in Illinois can care for a maximum of eight children (with some proscriptions on the age composition of the groups; up to twelve children may be cared for by the provider and an assistant; DCFS, 2003a; DHS, 2004). Some home-based providers should be licensed, but are not, sometimes because of lack of awareness or understanding of the licensing regulations. In licensed family day-care homes in Chicago and its surrounding counties, full-time care for infants averages $129 per week and full-time care for three-year-olds averages $119 per week. In the least populous counties of the state, licensed full-time care in private homes averages $78 per week for infants and averages $73 per week for three-year-olds. These amounts translate to between $3,500 and $6,500 per year for 50 weeks of care (author calculations based on Table 13 of DHS, 2003). The average cost of license-exempt care is unknown, but research suggests that such arrangements can require the fewest out-of-pocket costs for parents (e.g., relatives sometimes provide care at no monetary cost to parents; Anderson, Ramsburg, and Rothbaum, 2003).

indicator of the health of local child care markets. Needs assessments can help identify potential shortages, but cannot determine why such shortages exist and what policy responses will best address them. Needs assessments can also be misinterpreted if their methodological and conceptual assumptions are not well understood.

To help policymakers understand the underlying mechanisms of child care markets, we first present the economic perspective on shortages in child care. We then discuss the methodology of needs assessment analyses and the limitations of this approach. Finally, we discuss policies that could increase the use of licensed care in Illinois, including Illinois' ongoing development of a universal preschool system, or "Preschool for All."

The Economics of Child Care

According to economic theory, whether a child is in licensed care, unlicensed care, or at home with a parent is determined by the interaction of prices, preferences, market equilibria, and market failures (Blau, 2001). We discuss each of these factors in turn.

Price

Generally, license-exempt care is cheapest, followed by licensed home-based care and center care. In fact, center-based care is quite expensive in Illinois, as elsewhere. When they foot the full bill, parents are likely to spend more on center-based care for their young child than they will pay to send that child to college. Parental care also comes at a financial cost to the family, if it prevents the parent from working. The implicit cost is the parent's forgone wage. As a consequence, economic theory predicts that lower-wage parents (usually but not always the mother) will be more likely to drop out of the labor force in order to care for children.

The price of care influences demand. Child care is just one of many items that families wish to buy, and a family's income level sets a ceiling on their purchasing opportunities. Child care expenditures will limit the feasibility of other important purchases as well as inhibit the family's ability to save for future expenses, such as a home or their children's further education.

The price of care also influences its supply. Providers are constrained by the prices of inputs (e.g., wages paid to child care workers) and technology (e.g., advances in knowledge about early childhood development). These inputs and technology determine the relationship between price and supply. Holding technology constant, when the costs of inputs increase, profits decline, sometimes so low that the provider can no longer continue to offer care.

Preferences

Not every parent, when confronted with the same prices and income, will make the same child care choice. Each parent is assumed to have preferences for certain goods over others. Such preferences vary across parents. Some parents might be willing to offset the cost of buying another hour of child care by spending less on another good in their "basket" of consumption items. For example, one middle income family might forgo buying a new car so that their children can get more of the social or learning benefits that they perceive to be associated with higher-cost center care. Another family may be less likely to trade off other things to pay for center care because they view center care as providing comparable social and learning benefits as a family day care provider in their neighborhood. Preferences thus determine the relationship between price and demand. Holding income levels constant, if preferences shift, the amount of child care demanded at a given price will also change.

Market Equilibria and Child Care Shortages

Economic theory assumes and empirical evidence confirms that, for most goods, as price increases, supply goes up and demand goes down. As a consequence, if we begin at a price of zero, where demand exceeds supply, and then increase price, at some point we will find a price at which the quantity supplied equals the quantity demanded. This is an equilibrium. If the price differs from this equilibrium price, the market will move toward the equilibrium. That is, shortages (demand greater than supply) and surpluses (supply greater than demand) are eliminated through market forces. For example, if the price is at a point where the number of children whose parents can afford care exceeds the number of child care slots, then the price will go up. When this happens, supply and demand will move toward each other as more providers can operate profitably at the new price but fewer parents will be able to pay the new price. Likewise, if there are more slots available than children whose parents can afford care, then the price will decline. Supply and demand will move toward each other as some providers will leave the market (stop offering care) because they can no longer operate profitably at the lower price, and some parents will be able to afford care at the new price. (See Box 2 for additional discussion of affordability).

Box 2: What Is Affordable Care?

It is useful to pause and consider what it means to say that a parent can "afford care." Applying the economic principles just reviewed, being able to "afford care" means that a family will pay a given price for care, given the family's preferences and income level. Some parents may literally be unable to afford a certain type of care. That is, their income is so low and the cost of care so high that all "baskets" containing that care are out of their reach. For example, some private nanny care costs upwards of $450 per week. Fifty weeks of such care would cost $22,500. Families who earns less than this amount per year literally cannot afford this kind of care. As the price of care falls below the family's income level, there comes a point at which the family could pay for the care if they traded off other goods in their basket. It is at this point that the term "afford care" becomes more contentious. Economists tend to view this situation more positively than others may, since parents are viewed as optimizing their well-being (utility) by purchasing the basket of goods that they most prefer, given their budget constraint. Still, economists may agree that at some point government intervention is justified to help parents purchase care that they cannot afford for reasons of social equity or social good, as we discuss the interpretation of needs assessments.

Once achieved, the equilibrium price (and demand and supply) will remain until changes occur to the market (something that shifts preferences, the cost of inputs, or technology). The degree to which providers can respond to such market changes depends on the extent to which their inputs are fixed or variable. For fixed inputs, the quantity used cannot change much in a given time period (e.g., constructing a larger building or renting larger space). Variable inputs can change in the given time period (e.g., hiring additional staff). In the short run, some inputs are fixed. In the long run, all inputs are variable. Thus, in the long run, economic theory predicts that a provider can adjust completely to a change in the environment.

In a well-functioning market, there is really no such thing as a "shortage" of center care slots, strictly speaking. Rather, at prevailing prices, all those who find center care a financially feasible and desirable choice use it, while all providers supplying center care are at least able to cover their variable costs. From the economic perspective, the fact that many more parents would choose center care if it were less expensive relative to other modes does not constitute an intrinsic failure of the market to meet community needs for center care, as the supply and demand for center care

are in equilibrium (although this situation could be construed as a failure of government policy to support socially desirable outcomes). Note that a market-based view of child care is entirely compatible with a societal goal of increasing consumption of center care. That is, the fact that a market is in equilibrium is a separate issue from whether that equilibrium is socially optimal or desirable in some normative sense.

Market Failures

In real-world markets, however, it could actually be the case that at prevailing prices, there are parents who would choose center care but nevertheless are not observed using it. These "shortages" are produced by market failures. Market failures can occur on the supply or the demand side of the market. On the supply side, a provider may not build a new center because she cannot assure the minimum enrollment needed to raise the fixed capital. On the demand side, the "transaction costs" of searching for licensed care may be perceived to be too high for parents who can easily locate license-exempt care arrangements with friends or relatives. We next discuss how such failures may occur in the market for centers and home-based care.

Center Care. Center care generally requires significant startup costs (such as building or renovating a facility) and detailed pre-startup evaluations of viability. As a consequence, there could be true shortages in center care that persist for the period during which new centers are brought "on line." In such situations, there would be enough parents in the community willing to pay the provider's price to fill a new center, but these families would need to join waiting lists and make do with less preferred modes of care while they waited for a center to open. We consider two reasons for such short-run shortages: rapid population change and rapid changes in preferences. Shortages may also persist in the long run due to market failures. We discuss how concentrated poverty and low population density may create long-run gaps in center care availability.

Short-run misalignments between the number of center slots and the number of children in need of center-based care may be acute when an area experiences rapid population change. Due to the costs and logistics of opening a new center, supply of centers will lag behind the numbers of young children, even if incoming families desire center care and can pay for it. Population decline may result in the opposite problem, again reflecting the costs and logistics of centers. That is, when young children who grow up, or whose families move out of a community, are not replaced with newborns or families who move into a community, an existing center may find it difficult to keep enrollments (and prices) high enough to cover its costs. These population dynamics can result in a situation where, within a large geographic area like the Chicago metropolitan area or the State of Illinois, some communities may have an excess supply of centers and others may have insufficient supply. In addition to shifts in the actual number of children in the community, changes in preferences may also produce short-run shortages, for example, when maternal employment rises due to changes in welfare policy or when parents start to perceive licensed child care centers as offering higher quality social and learning benefits and begin seeking it in increasing numbers. Policy responses to short-run shortages may involve efforts to speed up the identification of shortages and surpluses and to facilitate the response of providers to these situations.

In some communities, shortages may persist in the long run due to an insufficient number of available parents who want and/or can afford center care. This is due to an "integer problem." Child care centers require a certain threshold number of children in order to operate and increases in the size of centers come in increments of additional classrooms rather than additional children. This constraint is in part due to state regulations that limit the maximum size of classrooms. When an additional child wants to enroll, the provider cannot add that child to an existing classroom that already meets the maximum size, but would instead need to open a new classroom. And, to remain profitable, a provider is unlikely to open (or keep open) a classroom that she cannot fill. This means that families that live in some areas may find it difficult to locate center care, even if they desire it and could personally afford to pay for it if they lived in a community that contained more families like themselves.

Such long-run gaps are particularly likely in low-income communities and in rural areas. In some low-income communities, parents may lack the financial resources to pay a high enough price to make a child care center profitable, even in the long run. That is, all market baskets that contain center care are beyond these families' budget constraints. Even if one or a small number of families in such communities have higher incomes, and could afford to pay a higher price to support this kind of care if they lived in a community populated by other parents with similar incomes, there will not be enough demand in the aggregate to support a center when most families in the area have lower incomes (e.g., a lone higher income parent would be better off paying for a highly trained nanny than the price it would take to support a center for one child). Indeed, for-profit child care centers are likely to target communities with demographic characteristics favorable to their enterprise (e.g., many middle- or higher-income dual-earner families). If entrepreneurs in some communities are discriminated against by lending institutions, there may also be a shortage of center care, for the simple reason that investment in a facility generally requires access to business credit. Due to the need for physical proximity, long-run gaps in availability may also occur when, consistently over time, only a small number of young children live close to a potential site for a center, such as in rural areas or in areas with certain demographic characteristics (primarily childless young adults or post-childrearing older persons and few young families).

Box 3: Size of the Child Care Market

Although different people may define the same market somewhat differently, clearly child care requires physical collocation of the child and provider. Thus, families generally only consider care that is located relatively close to their home (or work) and providers serve only nearby families. In other words, while it can be debated whether families living in one Chicago community area, like Austin, will use care in a neighboring community, like Oak Park, it is clear that families in Chicago are not in the market for care in Springfield. Thus, characteristics of the local area determine the level of supply and demand. The same family may face substantially different choices when located in one community versus another very different community. (Indeed, some families make seek neighborhoods because of the resources available for their family, including child care options.) And, the same provider will be more or less viable in two different neighborhoods.

Various policy reactions to these long-run shortages are possible. Some might argue that families with higher incomes who live in communities lacking a critical mass of families like themselves should move to areas with better supply of the kind of care that they prefer. Others might argue that access to center care is socially beneficial and government intervention is required. For example, income subsidies in low-income areas would circumvent parents' budget constraints, allowing them to access baskets of goods that contain center care. The consequent aggregate demand for care would allow a center provider to assure viability. Transportation support in rural areas might allow enough children to reach a provider to support her enterprise (or, alternatively, strategies might be devised to bring some of the social and learning benefits of center care to the child). We discuss these and other options further below as we discuss social equity and social benefits in relation to interpreting needs assessments.

Home-based Care. Because the entry and operating costs of home-based care are generally quite low, fewer shortages of this type of care are expected. The integer problem just discussed is less likely for home-based providers, since most run small operations or provide care temporarily, while their own children are young or to help out family or friends. These providers can respond quickly to changes in demand and can offer care in communities where only a small number of families demand it. They also generally offer care at a lower price than do centers, making them more accessible to lower income families. There are some exceptions to this situation, including cases in which home-based providers operate larger facilities, cases in which the local demographics provide few potential home-based providers, and cases in which parents have small personal networks.

Some providers who run larger licensed programs or who view caregiving as a long-term career may be more similar to centers. They may invest substantially in their homes to create spaces designed for child care (e.g., finishing an extra room or basement with shelving for toys and a sink for hand washing) and may belong to a local network of providers and have substantial ties to local information and activity resources (e.g., parks, libraries). Such investments in the operation may make it difficult to move in the event that their community population shifts away from young children. And, a provider may be reluctant to make investments to expand her program unless she can assure enough demand in the long run. Shortages in these larger scale and more professionalized home-based providers require similar policies as those discussed for centers above.

Other providers, particularly family, friend, and neighbor providers who care for one or a small number of children, are better able to move easily in and out of care provision as the need arises among nearby parents. However, the demographics of the local area and the size of personal networks limit access to this kind of care. Most child care providers are women. As more and more women enter the paid labor force they will be less available to provide caregiving services to family, friends, and neighbors. In such situations, potential caregivers must weigh the advantages of providing care (e.g., being able to watch their own children at home while taking care of a neighbor's children) with the advantages of working for pay in another occupation (e.g., higher pay, access to health care benefits, accumulation of seniority). Similarly, the supply of some kinds of caregivers, such as nannies who provide care in the child's home, may be greater in some communities than others (e.g., communities with large numbers of immigrant women). And, personal networks drive access to family, friend, and neighbor care because they are frequently located through word-of-mouth and involve nonmonetary exchanges (Anderson, Ramsburg, and Rothbaum, 2003). Two parents who live in the same community may have a very different slate of potential caregivers if one parent has many friends, family, and close neighbors in the area while another parent has few family and friends and little contact with neighbors.

A number of policy initiatives might address shortages in home-based care. Policymakers can facilitate the entry of new caregivers to the market when demand increases by providing information about starting a new family day care home. Caregivers can be attracted to stay in or move into caregiving rather than other occupations through offering benefits, like health care, and higher wages. Policies and programs can also be designed to help parents identify home-based care options. For example, family day care homes are less visible than are child care centers, and efforts to increase their listing with referral programs and outreach to parents to use such referral services may help match parents with desired caregivers.

Needs Assessments and Their Interpretations

In the last decade, concerns about whether children have equal access to developmentally-stimulating care and about why certain kinds of care are used more than others coincided with a recognition of the research possibilities of data collected for other purposes, primarily Child Care Resource and Referral Agency and U.S. Census Bureau data. Consequently, attempts to estimate the supply and demand of child care in communities around the country have increased. Such estimates have been characterized as tools for state, city, and local leaders in setting priorities and policies. In this section we provide examples of such needs assessments in Illinois. We then critique them in two ways: (1) are they accurately identifying shortages and (2) assuming they are accurate, how should they be interpreted? In doing so, we use concepts from the economic perspective outlined above.

Examples of Needs Assessments

Needs assessments in Illinois illustrate their methodology and use. The idea is straightforward: Identify a child care market, count the number of children who need care, count the number of slots of available child care, and compare the two in percentage or absolute terms. Putting this idea into practice is complicated by questions about how to define the market, which children to consider in need of care, and what slots to count.

The Illinois Facilities Fund has been a principal producer of needs assessments in Illinois. In the late 1990s, they published a widely-used needs assessment of child care in Chicago, a major impetus for the City of Chicago's Children's Capital Fund, which invested in new or expanded child care centers in the city's neediest communities (Illinois Facilities Fund, no date, 1999, 2004b). In 2004, the Illinois Facilities Fund released a statewide needs assessment of Illinois counties and municipalities (Illinois Facilities Fund, 2004a). Although this recent report does not update the Fund's earlier work on communities within Chicago, the City has supported continued estimates of community needs. For example, Chapin Hall Center for Children has been examining supply and demand for child care for the City of Chicago (Chapin Hall Center for Children, 2005).

The Illinois Facilities Fund's 1999 needs assessment identified Chicago communities with high unmet need for full-day licensed care of low-income infants, toddlers, and preschoolers (South Lawndale, Logan Square, New City, Englewood, West Ridge, Brighton Park, Hermosa, Lower West Side, Albany Park, Humboldt Park, West Englewood, Belmont Cragin, West Town, Gage Park, Avondale, Lincoln Square, Chicago Lawn, North Lawndale, McKinley Park, and Rogers Park). For example, in five communities (South Lawndale, Logan Square, New City, Brighton Park, and Hermosa), licensed, full-day slots were available for just three percent or fewer of the low-income children in need of care. The families in these communities tend to be very low-income, and the communities are majority Latino, majority African American, or mixed Latino and African American.

The City of Chicago's Children's Capital Fund invested in building or renovating child care facilities in these areas (Illinois Facilities Fund, 2004b).

The Illinois Facilities Fund's statewide needs assessment identified the areas most in need of care across the state, including ten municipalities (Cicero, Berwyn, Aurora, Bolingbrook, Mount Prospect, Calumet City, Elgin, Waukegan, Chicago Heights, and Chicago) and ten counties (Kane, Boone, Will, Suburban Cook, La Salle, DuPage, Shelby, Grundy, Montgomery, and Lake). For example, in Cicero there were slots available for only 13% of young children estimated to be in need of care. The Illinois Facilities Fund's statewide needs assessment also demonstrates the idea discussed above that because of the requirement of physical collocation of providers and children it is possible to have apparent shortages in some geographic areas and apparent surpluses in others. For example, while at the state level the Illinois Facilities Fund finds that there are more three-to-five-year-old children than full-day slots (194,999 children for 121,542 slots), in 17 municipalities, there are more slots than children (Belleville, Bloomington, Champaign, DeKalb, Des Plaines, East St. Louis, Elk Grove Village, Granite City, Highland Park, Mundelein, Naperville, Niles, Peoria, Quincy, Schaumburg, Springfield, and Urbana, Illinois Facilities Fund, 2004a, p. 65).

Do Needs Assessments Accurately Capture Child Care Shortages?

One approach to interpreting the needs assessments is to critique their definitions of the market, who is in need of care, and who is providing care. As we do so, it is important to keep in mind that some assumptions must be made about each of these definitions in order for needs assessments to be conducted. The Illinois needs assessments have improved their assumptions over time and have been quite transparent about their methodologies, generally clearly placing their assumptions front-and-center. Still, time-pressed decision makers may set aside these details to get to the findings. Thus, it is important to highlight these assumptions and how they might affect the results.

For example, the definition of the child care market affects needs assessments. Variation in unmet need among smaller units (e.g., cities) can be masked when needs assessments are conducted for larger areas (e.g., states). This point was illustrated above. In Chicago, there is also anecdotal evidence that the movement of former public housing residents has left some Head Start programs without a critical mass of eligible families nearby and some families distant from the nearest Head Start program. As such, there are empty slots in some programs while some families cannot find slots.[2] In addition, counting the number of slots and number of children in an area may be misleading if a community's supply is being used by families in a neighboring community.

Another important issue is who to define as in need of care and which slots to count in the supply of care. Altering assumptions about who needs and offers care can greatly affect needs assessments. For example, suppose we focus on three-year-old children, and consider three scenarios. In the first scenario, only licensed, center-based slots are counted as the supply, and all three-year-old children are counted as potentially in need of care. In the second scenario, we add licensed, home-based providers to the supply. In the third, we return to licensed, center-based care as the supply, but consider only children in single-parent/single-earner or two-parent/dual-earner families as in need of care. Clearly, the conclusions about unmet need will vary under these different scenarios. It is particularly difficult to know how to handle supply of and demand for license-exempt "family, friend, and neighbor care." Leaving out these providers ignores an important portion of the child care market. Doing so, might overstate the lack of care in a community, particularly if parents prefer these smaller, home-based forms of care. Yet, it is extremely difficult to count the supply of such care.[3]

When decision makers consider the need for particular programs, such as Head Start, ISBE pre-k, and subsidized child care, calculations need to focus the numerator on slots in the relevant program and the denominator on children eligible for the program. A complication in the case of early care and education programs (Head Start, ISBE pre-k, and subsidized child care) is that, while the exact eligibility requirements differ across the programs, some children are eligible for more than one program. If three separate needs calculations are made, and such children are counted as in need of each program, then too many slots may be opened. On the other hand, as noted above, Head Start and ISBE pre-k have traditionally been part-day programs, and sometimes providers blend funding streams, using two slots, each in a part-day program, to provide a full day of care for a child.

The sensitivity of results to assumptions about who is in need of and who is supplying care is particularly important as Illinois moves toward universal preschool. Because universal preschool initiatives aim to make organized early childhood education opportunities available, often with regulations aimed at assuring high quality (such as educational requirements for teachers and class size limitations), the numerator should be restricted to a very particular set of "high quality" slots. In addition, universal preschool aims to make preschool available to "all parents who wish to use it." Since it is quite difficult to identify who "wishes to use it," it is difficult to define the level of demand. In part this is because current usage patterns reflect current supply and demand and cannot predict whether parents might use new early education options if they were available. In addition, universal preschool initiatives may alter parental preferences since they are predicated on the evidence that high-quality early learning experiences better prepare children for school. Parents may adopt a preference for using preschool as they see more programs open and as more of their friends and neighbors use them.

One potential solution to concerns about the sensitivity of needs assessments' conclusions to definitions of the market, supply, and demand is to produce needs assessments that provide a range of estimates based on a range of assumptions. Any particular needs assessment has limited resources, and any individual or organization may be inclined toward particular assumptions. Thus, we also recommend that data sharing be facilitated so that researchers can easily apply alternative assumptions. Data sharing is particularly important because the information needed to conduct needs assessments are drawn from multiple sources and are time-consuming to collect and prepare. Some of the data may be viewed as confidential, and restricted-access data-sharing agreements might be required. Alternatively, government entities and foundations might support a web-based structure in which alternative assumptions could be applied "on the fly" so that a decision maker could readily see the results based on their preferred assumptions. Technology increasingly makes such options possible. Making information available about the residence of children who fill slots could also reveal whether children cross geographic boundaries for care.[4]

Interpreting Needs Assessments

Suppose agreement could be reached on a set of assumptions. How then should we interpret the resulting evidence that some communities have more children than slots (shortages) and some more slots than children (surpluses)? We focus our attention on policies to remedy shortages, since they have been a focal point of public and policy dialogue. We organize our discussion into three sections. First, if parents want and can afford care, no or limited action may be needed, although some policies might accelerate the establishment and expansion of caregivers consistent with parents' desires. Second, if parents want but cannot afford certain kinds of care, policies can subsidize that form of care. Most often, subsidies take the form of government-funded slots, vouchers, and individual tax breaks. Third, if parents don't wa nt certain kinds of care that society deems desirable, public awareness campaigns may be used to promote them. The government can also more directly promote certain kinds of care through differential subsidies and increased regulation, such as by locating preschool programs within public schools or contracting with community providers to deliver highly prescribed forms of care.

Parents Want and Can Afford Care. Short-run shortages reflect situations where parents want and can afford care, but the market is out of equilibrium. As noted above, economic theory suggests that the market will resolve such temporary imbalances on its own. Economists might argue that point-in-time needs assessments accentuate the need for policy interventions when in fact, left alone, the market might adjust itself to these short-run supply and demand imbalances.

Still, it is possible that needs assessment might helpfully accelerate market responses, particularly in situations where rapid population change has produced imbalance. In some cases, the needs assessments themselves may produce sufficient attention to help providers identify communities that are undergoing rapid population increases as good locations for new centers.

103

In others, additional public strategies may be needed to encourage new or expanded centers, or the move of a provider from an area of population loss to an area of population gain (e.g., capital investments, provider training), although again needs assessments might help target such initiatives.

Another alternative to the problem of shortages in some areas and surpluses in others is to help families better match with communities that offer the kinds of care that they desire. Initiatives like those described above that make the information underlying needs assessments readily available would support such family decision making. Such an approach could be implemented by encouraging resource and referral agencies to make information about the supply of child care more accessible and detailed. At present, information ranges from online, searchable databases with information about provider education and training to call in for a list of providers in the area with information limited to name, address, and phone number.

Parents Desire But Cannot Afford Care. Other imbalances in supply and demand may reflect long-run shortages and surpluses. As noted, many of the areas identified as in highest need of center care in Illinois are the lowest-income, minority communities that may require government subsidies because parents cannot afford to pay a high price for center care, even if they want it. For example, a single parent earning the minimum wage who worked 40 hours per week for 50 weeks of the year would earn $13,000. The average cost for 50 weeks of full-time center care in Chicago is $6,800 for a three-year-old and $10,000 for an infant (Illinois Department of Human Services, 2003).

Illinois' existing subsidy program is already designed to help such parents afford center care. Thus, on the one hand, shortages could reflect the fact that subsidy-eligible families don't want to use center -based care (more on this in a moment). On the other hand, the absence of providers in such low-income communities may reflect the structure of Illinois' subsidy system, including its below-market reimbursement rates, high co-payments, and steep changes in child care costs when parents' earnings become too high to continue in the program.

Regarding the structure of the subsidy program, economic theory predicts that when government intervention imposes a price ceiling, a shortage will result. If we impose a maximum amount that providers can charge, such as through maximum reimbursement rates under the subsidy program, and this price is below the equilibrium point, then there will be more parents who would like to purchase care at this price than providers willing to offer care. In addition, if the ceiling price is below the price that providers need to cover the costs of high quality care, they may cut corners and reduce quality in order to stay in business. To the extent that parents can observe such cost cutting, they may not utilize these lower-quality settings. State market rate surveys suggest that the reimbursement rates in Illinois are indeed ceilings, generally not meeting the federal recommendation of providing access to at least 75% of local providers. In some cases, the differential is dramatic. For example, for children over two and a half in Chicago-area counties, over two-thirds of area providers charge a rate higher than the state reimbursement rate (Illinois Department of Human Services, 2003, Figure 19). In the recent tight budget climate, the state has not revised reimbursement rates, although advocates have recently increased their pressure on state lawmakers to increase the reimbursement rates in Illinois and to institute a tiered reimbursement rate that would provide incentives to increase the quality of care settings (Illinois Department of Human Services, 2005).

The fact that reimbursement rates are too low to provide access to many providers may keep some eligible parents from signing up for the program. Eligibility and co-payment rules in Illinois may also decrease participation in the program. Advocates have highlighted the considerable "cliff" in the amount parents pay for child care when they move over the income eligibility level for subsidies. For example, consider a single mother with one three-year-old child using center care in Cook County. In FY 2006, if her monthly income increases by one dollar to $2,052 per month and she began paying the full amount the state was paying for care, she jumps from paying one-tenth to nearly one-quarter of her monthly income on child care (see also Alexander and Stoll, 2004, p. 18). This is because the average cost of center-based care is high. The amounts noted above for Chicago-area centers ($10,000 per year for infant and toddler care and nearly $7,000 per year for preschooler care) are approximately one-half to two-thirds of the 2002 federal poverty guideline of $15,020 for a family of three. They are also comparable to or higher than what it would cost to send a child to college, for example, being about 2-3 times higher than the average cost of tuition in 2000-2001 for in-state undergraduates at Illinois public universities ($3,807).

Even when a family's income is below the eligibility limit, the co-payment rates in Illinois are relatively high. For example, Illinois is one of only thirteen states that require non-employed TANF parents to make a co-payment and it ranks near the middle of states in the level of co-payment for a family of three. The federal government recommends that co-payments never exceed 10% of income, although Illinois' co-payments in some cases do. In Illinois, a single parent with one child pays between 1% and 10% of her gross income on the child care co-payment while a single parent with two children pays up to 15% of her gross income on the co-payment. The co-payment remains the same regardless of the number of providers used or the type of care selected by the parent and the co-payment is collected by the provider. Although hard numbers do not exist, anecdotal evidence suggests that some providers, especially family, friend, and neighbor caregivers, don't require parents to make the co-payment. This practice makes economic sense for the provider, particularly if the parent's income is quite low and the co-payment is quite low, since the bulk of the provider's payment comes from the state. Yet, this practice would further exacerbate the cost differential between center-based and family, friend and neighbor care and may encourage such parents to use family, friend and neighbor care.

Parents' Dont Want Care. When interpreting needs assessments, many have asked whether parents simply prefer small, home-based care settings, especially for their infants and toddlers. This question is difficult to answer. In part, this is because preferences are difficult to measure. Prior studies of preferences in Illinois suggest that more parents prefer center care than use it. However, like other studies of preferences, these studies can be

Box 4: The Push For Early Childhood Education

In the 1990s, a trend began toward making preschool available for all three- and four-year-olds whose parents wished to use it. Some states began to expand eligibility for preschool programs that traditionally served at-risk (low-income) children. Georgia created the first universal program, providing access to all children, in 1995 (Barnett et al., 2004).

These initiatives are based, in part, on the evidence that early childhood education can help prepare poor children for school. Numerous small-scale randomized studies, and several more recent large-scale experiments, find short- and long-term benefits of such early interventions (Barnett and Hustedt, 2005). Caution is warranted in extending these findings to state policy initiatives, however.

First, little evidence exists on what curriculum is most beneficial, although evaluated early childhood education programs are considered to be on the high end of quality. In contrast, quality is much more variable, and lower on average, in community child care settings (Fuller, Kagan, Loeb, and Chang, 2004). One review reports that early childhood education programs typically have effects that are two to four times larger than the average child care center (Brooks-Gunn, 2004). Thus, universal preschool initiatives should not lose their focus on requirements to support quality (e.g., teacher credentials and wages; curricular guidance and support). And, the push toward universal preschool should not be extended to a push toward center-based care per se (without attention to quality). Indeed, there is some evidence of negative outcomes for child behavior and physical health associated with more time spent in large child care settings (Gordon et al., 2005; NICHD Early Child Care Research Network, 2003).

Second, most interventions have targeted low-income children, making it difficult to determine the benefits of preschool for higher-income children. Spending money on universal access may be of less societal benefit than spending money on access for at-risk children, particularly if middle-income families are more likely to enroll in voluntary, high-quality, publicly-funded preschool programs but their children are less likely to benefit from it. Some research suggests that the benefits of early childhood education are stronger for lower-income children (Brooks-Gunn, 2004; Gormley and Phillips, 2005), although others do not (Burchinal et al., 2000).

Third, there is little research on how much preschool experience is needed to prepare children for school. Thus, policymakers have little evidence on which to base decisions to offer full-day versus half-day programs (although there is a larger literature on part-day versus full-day kindergarten; Loeb et al., 2005[§]). And, although home-visiting interventions, in which parents are provided training and support in their homes, have generally not found positive effects on child outcomes, there has not been a systematic attempt to offer the same or similar curriculum as found in center-based early child education in home-based settings, including family day care. Indeed, in contrast to center-based early childhood education, home visiting traditionally has focused on supporting and enhancing parenting behaviors, rather than readying children for school per se. It is possible that intensive home-based school-readiness interventions would show positive results. One recent study found that children had higher cognitive scores when their families had received more intensive versus less intensive parenting services during home visits (Brooks-Gunn, 2004).

The current tides toward universal preschool generally privilege more formalized options for child care. Wrap-around efforts have focused on center-based options over the more logistically challenging possibilities of combining home-based care with part-day preschool (Schumacher et al., 2005). Yet, dedicated preschool facilities where children are brought to the site are costly, particularly as outlined above when the population of young children shifts over time. Alternative strategies might build from existing community facilities and networks of care to "take the enrichment to the child." The possibility that early care and education might be flexibly offered in home-based settings is thus an attractive option, but one that has received less policy and research attention. The Illinois Early Learning Council recently conducted focus groups to develop recommendations for family child care providers' participation in Preschool for All, including through transporting children to and from preschool, bringing in teachers to offer preschool-like activities in a neighborhood home, or family day care providers achieving the qualifications needed to offer preschool activities themselves (Margie Wallen, personal communication, October 27, 2005). Such models deserve more attention and evaluation.

easily critiqued. For example, parents must often trade off their own needs for affordable and convenient care with the ideal setting for their child's developmental needs, and they may feel uncomfortable revealing to researchers that parental needs are considered. Relatedly, parents are often asked to rank the importance of separate characteristics of providers, like their location, cost, training, education, and child caregiver relationship, when in fact they usually choose among a limited set of options that "bundle" together various characteristics, making it unlikely that parents will find their exact "ideal" configuration of characteristics in their community. And, the degree to which often-used hypothetical questions, such as "If cost was not a concern, what type of care would you choose?" are informative about actual decisions parents might make is unknown.

It is also the case that surveys of current usage patterns reflect the current supply of child care options and cannot predict how parents' behavior might change when new options are introduced. This problem is particularly acute when needs assessments are used to justify new initiatives, such as universal preschool, since they cannot predict how parents' behavior, and that of other local providers, may change when a new option becomes available. Public initiatives to build more child care facilities provide "natural experiments" to study changes in usage patterns when new options are introduced. In Illinois, the Chicago Children's Capital Fund was a public-private partnership, including the City of Chicago and Illinois Facilities Fund, that built or expanded child care facilities to 20 low-income communities. However, to our knowledge this initiative has not been systematically evaluated. Other studies suggest that unanticipated changes in parental behavior can result from new policies. An evaluation of the Georgia program notes that "The population of families and children served by private preschools in Georgia has been affected significantly by the options for parents to enroll their children in Georgia Pre-K. . ."[5] (Henry et al., 2003, p. 4). Indeed, under universal preschool initiatives, it is possible that some middle-income families would shift from private-pay to public-pay preschool (and increase costs for the state) at the same time that a substantial number of low-income families could remain unserved because they do not

108

voluntarily enroll. Such findings lend support to the Illinois Governor's Task Force on Universal Access to Preschool's recommendations for sliding fees and statewide outreach campaigns. (See Box 4 for additional discussion of universal preschool)

As noted, needs assessments also often assume that families will not decide that they are better off having one parent withdraw from the labor market partially or completely in order to provide care. Indeed, there may be a point at which it is more cost effective for the government to support parents staying home to raise children rather than subsidizing high-cost, high-quality care. Still, such a conclusion would be politically unlikely without reversing the great societal shift about cash assistance and maternal employment that led to the welfare-to-work reforms of the 1990s. Indeed, some might argue that the consequent gaps in parental labor force experience, lowered family income, and possible need for government cash assistance are not desirable. They might also argue that particularly for three- and four-year-olds, government support for high-quality preschool programs will have a substantial payoff in terms of children's school readiness and adult productivity.

Conclusions

Needs assessments are potentially useful descriptions of current patterns of child care use in a defined geographic area. A needs assessment may be a good first screen for identifying areas in which use of particular kinds of care is low. However, a needs assessment provides no information on why this is the case. To give one example, in a very wealthy area, the use of center care may be extremely low because many families use even more expensive nanny care. In a neighboring poor area, the use of center care may be extremely low because center care is more expensive than license-exempt care and child care subsidies do not provide adequate incentives for center care to be available and used. Identifying the mechanisms that underlie the apparent shortages identified by needs assessments requires that supplementary evidence be obtained.

Child care policy prescriptions will also vary depending on the source of the problem. Capital market constraints in poor areas may be

109

appropriately addressed by special loan programs or direct capital investment in facilities. Alternatively, if transaction and information costs are an issue, child care resource and referral agencies and community outreach efforts may play an important role in increasing the use of center care. Finally, if center care is simply too expensive for many, further reductions in the relative price can be obtained through changes to the state's subsidy structure.

As discussed above, we encourage the continued improvement and transparency of assumptions on which needs assessments are based and wider use and dissemination of the data that support needs assessments. Doing so will assure that calculations are most appropriate to particular policy questions and that results are interpreted correctly. We also encourage continued study of why apparent shortages exist (through further study of parents' decision-making processes), how families react to policy interventions (such as evaluations of capital investments in new facilities), and demonstration projects to explore innovative policies (such as strategies for engaging home-based providers in "Preschool for All").

References

Alexander, David and Marcia Stoll. 2004. *Elements of Child Care Supply and Demand: 2004 Report on Child Care in Cook County.* Chicago, IL: Action for Children.

Anderson, Steven G., Dawn M. Ramsburg, and Bari Rothbaum. 2003. *Illinois Study of License-Exempt Child Care: Interim Report.* at http://www.dhs.state.il.us/newsPublications/plansReports/pdfs/dhs_plan Reports_isleccir.pdf

Barnett, W. Steven, Jason T. Hustedt, Kenneth B. Robin, and Karen L. Schulman. 2004. *The State of Preschool: 2004 State Preschool Yearbook.* New Brunswick, NJ: The National Institute for Early Education Research.

Barnett, W. Steven and Jason T. Hustedt. 2005. Head Start's lasting benefits. *Infants and Young Children,* 18(1), 16-24.

Blau, David M. 2001. *The Child Care Problem: An Economic Analysis.* New York: Russell Sage Foundation.

Brooks-Gunn, J. 2004. Intervention and policy as change agents for young children. Pages 293-340 in P. Lindsay Chase-Lansdale, K. Kiernan, & R. J. Friedman (Eds). *Human Development Across Lives and Generations: The Potential for Change.* New York: Cambridge University Press.

Burchinal, Margaret R., Ellen Peisner-Feinberg, Donna M. Bryant, and Richard Clifford. 2000. Children's social and cognitive development and child care quality: Testing for differential associations related to poverty, gender, or ethnicity. *Applied Developmental Science*, 4(3), 149-165.

Chapin Hall Center for Children. 2005. *Early Childhood Programs Supply and Demand.* at http://dcys-ccsd.chapinhall.org/

Chicago Partners for Children. 2003. "Early Care and Education in Chicago: Bringing Families and Resources Together," at http://www.daycare-action.org/_uploads/documents/live/EarlyCare_and_Education_in-_Chicago.pdf

Fuller, Bruce, Sharon Lynn Kagan, Susanna Loeb, and Yueh-Wen Chang. 2004. Child care quality: Centers and home settings that serve poor families. *Early Childhood Research Quarterly*, 19, 505-527.

Gordon, Rachel A., Robert Kaestner, and Sanders Korenman. 2005. *The Spread of Common Illnesses in Child Care: Variation by Type of Care, Consequences for Maternal Employment, and Effectiveness of Infection Control.* Chicago, IL: Institute of Government and Public Affairs.

Gormley, William T. and Deborah Phillips. 2005. The effects of universal pre-k in Oklahoma: Research highlights and policy implications. *The Policy Studies Journal*, 33(1), 65-82.

Henry, Gary T. et al. (2003). *Report of the Findings from the Early Childhood Study: 2001-2002.* Atlanta: Georgia State University.

Illinois Department of Children and Family Services. 2003. *Summary of Licensing Standards for Day Care Homes.* at http://www.state.il.us/-dcfs/docs/summdch.pdf

Illinois Department of Children and Family Services. 2004a. *Child Care Act Study Guide,* at http://www.state.il.us/DCFS/docs/CCActStudy.pdf

Illinois Department of Children and Family Services. 2004b. *Summary of Licensing Standards for Day Care Centers,* at http://www.state.il.us/-dcfs/docs/CFS105052.pdf

Illinois Department of Human Services. 2003. *FY 2002 Market Rate Survey of Child Care in Illinois,* at http://www.dhs.state.il.us/ts/pdf/-mrs.pdf

111

Illinois Department of Human Services. 2005. Rates Report. Available at http://www.dhs.state.il.us/newsPublications/plansReports/pdfs/dhs_child Care-RatesReport1-13-05.pdf

Illinois Department of Human Services. 2004. *2003 Report on Illinois Child Care,* at http://www.dhs.state.il.us/newsPublications/plansReports/pdfs/-dhs_planReports_iccar03.pdf

Illinois Facilities Fund. no date. *Early Childhood Care and Education Fact Book.* Available at http://www.iff.org/resources/content/2/6/documents/-Fact_Book.pdf

Illinois Facilities Fund. 1999. *Chicago Early Childhood Care and Education Needs Assessment* (Abridged version). Available at http://www.iff.org/resources/content/1/1/documents/City_Needs_Assess _Abr.pdf

Illinois Facilities Fund. 2004a. *Statewide Early Childhood Needs Assessment. Available* at http://www.iff.org/content.cfm?ContentAlias=-statewideneedsassess

Illinois Facilities Fund. 2004b. *Chicago Childrens Capita l Fund.* Available at http://www.iff.org/content.cfm/childrenscapfund

Loeb, Susanna, Margaret Bridges, Daphna Bassok, Bruce Fuller, and Russ Rumberger. Forthcoming. How much is too much? The influence of preschool centers on childrens development nationwid e. *Economics of Education Review.*

NICHD Early Child Care Research Network. 2005. Early child care and childrens development in the primary grades: Follow -up results from the NICHD Study of Early Child Care? *American Educational Research Journal*, 42(3), 537-570.

Schumacher, Rachel, Danielle Ewen, Katherine Hart, and Joan Lombardi. 2005. All together now: State experiences in using community-based child care to provide pre-kindergarten. *CLASP Policy Brief.* Washington, DC: Center for Law and Social Policy.

Notes

*This work originated when the authors co-organized a conference on "Illinois Child Care: Making Connections" that was funded by the John D. and Catherine T. MacArthur Foundation and by Partnership Illinois at the University of Illinois at Urbana-Champaign.

[1]In Illinois in FY2003, 29% of subsidized care took place in centers, 16% in licensed homes, and 55% in license-exempt homes (Illinois Department of Human Services 2004, page 5).

[2]Other factors also contribute to empty Head Start slots. Some argue, for example, that movement of poor families into the workforce through welfare reform has contributed to a decline in Head Start enrollments since families are not categorically eligible once off of TANF and, once working, their incomes may rise above the low eligibility criterion of the federal poverty line and they may need full-time care while many Head Start programs are part-time.

[3]Indeed, if we consider the parent as a possible caregiver, then it is possible to think of scenarios in which there would be no shortage of care. The arguments can become somewhat circular here, but this can be done in one of two principal ways. First, if we allow parental care to be on the supply side, then the parent could be a potential caregiver, if for example they withdrew from the labor force or chose a shift that did not coincide with the shift of a spouse, partner, family member, or friend. Second, if we restrict the supply side to non-parental care, the adjustment could be made to the demand side, noting that some parents who could withdraw from the labor force or adjust shifts do not really need care. Although such adjustments seem extreme, in fact the Illinois Facilities Fund is making such a demand side assumption based on current usage patterns (how many parents actually are out of the labor force and choose non-overlapping shifts).

[4]Importantly, these web-based resources should be defined such that the original source data are secure and such that only aggregate reports are provided that do not identify particular children in particular care settings.

[5]Quoted from page 4 of Henry, Gary T. et al. (2003). *Report of the Finding from the Early Childhood Study: 2001-2002*. Atlanta: Georgia State University.

§The Illinois Facilities Fund's assumptions about part-day versus full-day programs will make it likely to conclude unmet need for full-day care. That is, in assessing demand, they exclude part-day slots from their overall needs assessment and downweight primarily part-day Head Start and preschool slots in a composite needs indicator. In estimating the need for full-time Head Start, they also make an assumption that working parents need a full-day program, although some may work part-time or non-day shifts. See page 61 of statewide needs assessment These assumptions are important to decision makers. For example, in planning for universal preschool, if a local community has too many full-time preschool slots and too few part-time preschool slots, then the state may pay more than needed (if some who would have used part-time instead use full-time), take-up rates may be low (if some cannot, or will not, use full-time slots), and achieving universality might be delayed (if an "extra" full time slot could have better served two children as two part-day slots).

113

Chapter 8

*Assessing Illinois After-School Needs For Children and Families: A Data Driven Approach**

Peter Mulhall

"Youth need places and people to succeed."– Unknown

Background

Due to the changing nature of families, the economy, education, and demographics, the need for after-school programs has grown exponentially over the past decade. Moreover, a better understanding of the benefits of after-school programs for promoting youth development and reducing youth problem behaviors such as school failure and delinquency continues to emerge (Mulhall, Stone, and Stone, 1996; and Belle, 1999). Large-scale evidence of the impact of after-school programs on academic achievement is equivocal. Nevertheless, families, communities, and the general public strongly support funding for high quality after-school programming as a way to support families and positively influence children and youth (Riley, 1997; U.S. Department of Education, 2003). In fact, in 2001 the Illinois General Assembly passed HR63 and SR70 to create the Illinois After-School Initiative. This legislation charged the Illinois Board of Education and Illinois Department of Human Services to convene a task force to assess the status of Illinois after-school programs.

The Illinois Department of Human Services commissioned the Center for Prevention Research and Development to conduct three studies to (1) assess the need for after-school programs; (2) to assess the number of existing after-school programs in Illinois; and (3) to determine quality, best practices, and benefits of current Illinois after-school programs. This chapter

114

is based on the needs assessment study that the task force submitted.

The demand for after-school programs is contingent upon how one defines the needs of children, families, and communities. It is also based on the major goals and purposes of after-school programs. Multiple stakeholders including parents, educators, child advocates, law enforcement, and communities each have their own rationale for who needs after-school programs and what problems or issues such programs will address. Illustratively, the national organization of *Fight Crime: Invest in Kids*— comprised of more than 2,500 police chiefs, sheriffs, prosecutors, victims of violence, and police officer associations across the United States—released a study showing most juvenile crime occurs in the after-school hours of 3:00 - 7:00 p.m. This suggests that they believe after-school programs create unique opportunities to reduce crime and delinquency in many communities (Newman, Fox, Flynn, and Christeson, 2000). In contrast, the major goal of the U.S. Department of Education's 21st Century Community Learning Center is to promote educational enhancement and to reduce the achievement gap, particularly among disadvantaged populations. In 1997, the State of Illinois developed the Teen Responsibility, Education, Achievement and Caring, and Hope (Teen-REACH) program with a different goal in mind. This act was an effort to assist families and communities that were significantly affected by welfare reform in which a larger percentage of single mothers were required go to work or school (NGA, 1998).

These needs identified at the national, state, and local levels, are reinforced by a number of national and state opinion polls that report high levels and consistent support for after-school programs. Most families with children simply argue that it just makes sense to have children in supervised and enriched settings as compared to letting them hang out on the streets or stay home alone.

Illinois has a long tradition in offering after-school programs as part of the churches, school districts, YMCAs, Boys and Girls Clubs, Scouting, and numerous other types of youth services. In fact, in our assessment of current Illinois after-school programs, we found an after-school program that has been offering services for several years. Most child advocates and policymakers view after-school services as an integration and extension of high quality early childhood and child-care services. In the past decade or so, after-school programs have reached new heights for expectations with expanded goals and purposes such as improving educational attainment, positive youth development, safety, and reduction of high-risk behaviors such as substance abuse, teen pregnancy, and juvenile delinquency. Moreover, recent research also suggests that children and youth problems ranging from school failure to drug abuse to teen pregnancy can be prevented or delayed by youth participation in quality after-school programs (Richardson, Radziszewska, Dent, and Flay, 1993; Mahoney, Lord, and Carryl, 2005). Nonetheless, high-quality needs assessments for after-school programs, with the exception of child-care studies, are few and far between.

After-school programs are unique environments for creating opportunities, educational enhancements, and experiences into arts, music, recreation, life skills, mentors, prevention education, physical activity, culture, and a myriad of other pro-social qualities. Community needs and funding sources are the most common factors that drive program development. As a result, the need for after-school programs may be driven by parents, youth, law enforcement, schools, preventionists, sports teams, clubs, and other organizations. The remainder of this chapter is guided by the following questions:

1) What are the best estimates for after-school needs based on the Illinois youth population and targeted risk conditions?
2) What data sources are available to help to define or estimate the need for after-school services in Illinois?
3) What are the strengths and limitations of these data sources and how should these data be used to carefully guide the need-identification process at the state and local levels?

Data Sources

The three data sets used in this study are comprehensive, include a large numbers of Illinois children and families, and cover most of the state. These data sets include (1) U.S. Census data for Illinois (1990, 2000); (2) Illinois State Board Education's (ISBE) school report card and studen t achievement data; and (3) Illinois Youth Survey (IYS) data collected in 2002 by Chestnut Health Systems in Bloomington and funded by the Illinois Department of Human Services, Substance Abuse Prevention Program.

Needs Based on School-Age Youth Population

Results for the needs analysis reflect basic information culled from the three aforementioned data sets. Using the 2000 Census data, we began the analysis by classifying more than 1,300 Illinois communities into six population groups ranging from fewer than 2,500 residents to greater than 250,000. We also wanted to determine where growth was occurring. Figure 1 shows the overall growth rate of the six groups of Illinois communities since the last decennial census, and the corresponding growth rates for youth between the ages of 6 and 17. The most apparent changes took place in communities with populations between 100,000 and 249,999 (Rockford, Peoria, Springfield, Joliet, Aurora, and Naperville), with an increase of 134% in youth over the past ten years. Of the six communities, it should be

Figure 1: Major Youth Population Change Areas for Youth, 1990-2000

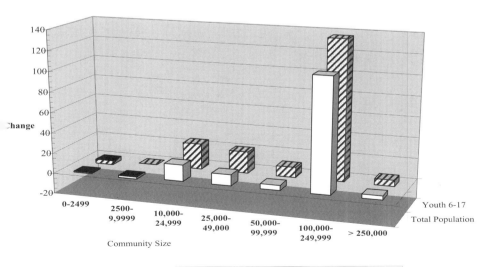

117

noted that Joliet, Aurora, and Naperville were the fastest growing. Most communities groups report modest growth (7–21%), while Chicago grew by 5%. Illinois' smallest communities actually experienced decreases in their youth populations by 4% from 1990 to 2000.

Needs Based on Family Structure and Circumstances

We also examined the family characteristics that likely are in greatest need of after-school services. Increases in need can be the result of changing family structures—particularly the growth of two-parent working families and large increases in single-parent families. Moreover, families in poverty are likely to lack the resources to purchase after-school services. Using the 2000 Census, we examined the number of families that have one parent or two parents in the workforce, as well as the number of families living in poverty. Figure 2 shows family structure data for the six Illinois community groupings. In nearly all of the communities, approximately 50% of the families have two parents, with the exception of Chicago, which is 28% two-parent. The proportion of single-parent families dramatically increases as the size of the community increases. Further, the number of single-parent families in poverty increases with the size of communities. More than one-fourth of Chicago's families are single -parent families living

Figure 2: Percentage of Youth in Family Types by Community Size

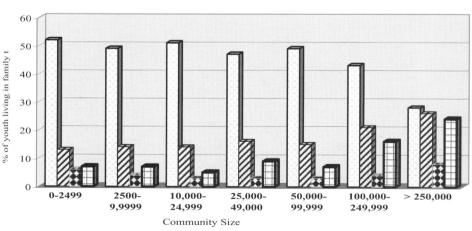

118

in poverty. These patterns suggest that higher proportions of Illinois' disadvantaged children who live in single-parent households and those living in poverty are disproportionately in Illinois'larger communities (greater than 100,000) compared with those in communities with less than 100,000 people. Finally, two-parent families in poverty are the least common family configuration across all community groups. Nevertheless, they should also be considered in the after-school mix to help provide adequate supervision and enrichment for these children and families.

Single-parent families and families in poverty are without question two groups that are most likely to need after-school programs and services (see Figure 2). When both parents work, whether in poverty or not, children may need after-school services due to significant amounts of unsupervised time or time they may have hanging out with friends. These risk factors are compounded in single-parent families in poverty, where fewer options are available because of the lack of resources, lack of transportation, lack of adult supervision, and lack of constructive places for children.

After-School Needs Based on Educational Failure

We also examined data from Illinois School Report Cards and the Illinois Student Achievement Tests (ISAT) to assess potential needs for after-school programs and services. These data show the number, types, and percentage of students who are not meeting Illinois academic standards. Along with the achievement data, we list several school characteristics that likely contribute to risk and result in academic failure.

A substantial body of research has reported school failure and attachment as part of a cluster of youth behaviors that include socio-emotional and behavioral problems (Jessor and Jessor, 1974; Resnick et al., 1997; Battistich, Schaps and Wilson, 2004). As a result, many researchers and educators believe that educational success is fundamentally and inextricably linked to becoming a healthy and productive adult citizen (Carnegie Council on Adolescent Development, 1989). There are, however, some differences in what approach should be used, particularly for those children living in poverty. Academic success has new meaning in Illinois with the roll out of the Illinois Standards for Learning in 1997, and the recent No Child Left Behind legislation, in which failing schools face serious consequences ranging from being placed on a watch list to undergoing reconfiguration.

We analyzed reading and math scores for students in grades 3, 5, and 8, since these are among the grades when children are likely to need after-school services. ISBE data allow us to examine after-school program needs based on the percentages of children who are not meeting Illinois academic standards for reading and mathematics. The assumption here is that after-school settings can provide appropriate settings for helping children who are not meeting Illinois state standards. In fact, the federally funded 21st Century Community Learning Centers was designed to support schools and communities to help them reach state standards.

The percentages of students not meeting Illinois standards for reading and math were 37% and 38% respectively, but the range of scores spanned from 10% to 91%, which shows extraordinary variation among Illinois schools and communities. Figure 3 shows that smaller communities

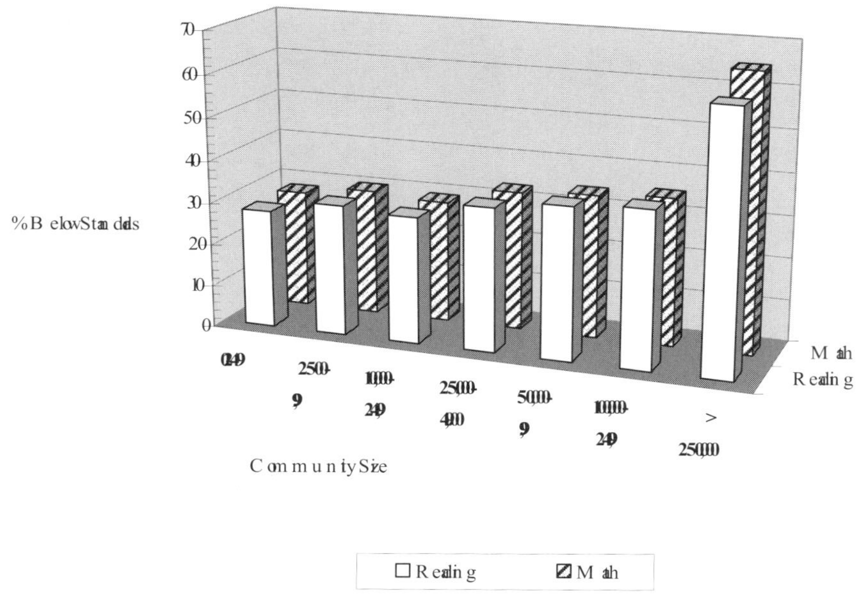

Figure 3. ISAT Scores for 3rd, 5th, and 8th Graders by Community Size

have fewer children not meeting state standards. It also shows that as community size increase, there are increases in the number of children not meeting standards. Chicago has twice the rate of students not meeting state standards as does Illinois' smallest communities.

The wide range of Illinois children not meeting the state's academic standards can be attributed to a number of community conditions ranging from poverty, low family involvement and expectations, little student mobility, poor teacher quality, and large numbers of students with limited English proficiency (LEPs) (National Assessment of Educational Progress, 1998).

After-School Needs Based on Self-Report of Latchkey Status

A third data source for this assessment was the Illinois Youth Survey (IYS), funded by the Illinois Department of Human Services, and conducted by Chestnut Health Systems, Bloomington (Markwood, McDermeit, and Godley, 2001). With more than 25,000 Illinois students, IYS provides a biennial "snapshot" of health -related behaviors, including a measure of children's self -report of time alone after school. In fact, the surveys asks students directly about the number of days they come to an "empty home" during a week, as well as the number hours they are home alone during the same one-week period. Using these two questions, we can calculate a composite score (number of days times the number of hours) that estimates the number of hours spent alone per week.

Our research suggests that the number of hours youth spend home alone is one of the critical factors related to high-risk problem behaviors and missed opportunities of school-age youth. That is, we found evidence that the emergence of youth problem behaviors is less a result of coming to an empty home, per se, than the length of time that a child spends home alone (Richardson, Radziszewska, Dent, and Flay, 1993; Mulhall, Stone, and Stone, 1996). To that end, we identified a time alone "threshold" for high - risk behaviors, which seem to appear when a child is alone at home for approximately 10 or more hours per week.

Figure 4: Percentage of Illinois Eigth Grade Students Reporting Latchkey Status by Community Size

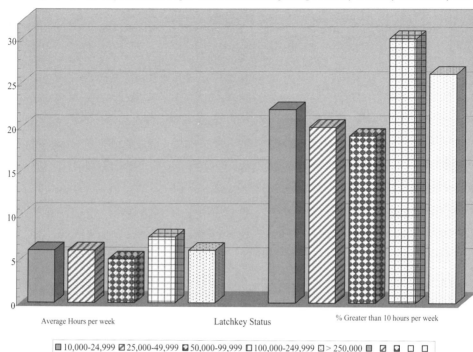

Using this threshold, we calculated statewide averages for the number of latchkey days and hours among 10,765 Illinois students in our 8th grade sample. Figure 4 shows that the average Illinois youth is home alone approximately six hours per week with a standard deviation of seven hours. The number of latchkey hours per week ranged from 0 to 23 hours (minimum and maximum on the survey scale). We found that 41% of 8th-grade students in Illinois were home alone more than 10 hours per week. These results show that most Illinois communities have about 20% of students home alone at least 10 hours per week. Again, larger Illinois communities have the highest percentages.

Summary and Recommendations

As described with these data, the need for after-school programs and services from a policy perspective largely depends upon how one defines the population in need or the targeted problem one is seeking to address. The potential needs are based on the expectations of what benefits could be derived from after-school programs viewed by parents, children themselves, stakeholders, policymakers, educators, community members, and funders. Most child and youth development advocates would argue for the universal approach in which all youth ages 6–17 would have access to affordable, high quality after-school programs that promote personal, social, and academic development and enrichment. We already know many Illinois youth participate in school and community-based programs supported by churches, youth groups, sports, arts and leisure organizations, park districts, scouting organizations, 4-H Extension, and numerous others. However, participation varies according to community location, availability, cost, quality, and interest. To that end, most youth participate in after-school programs because their families want them to or because after-school programs can be educational and exciting places to be with friends and family members.

Several important observations can also be made about the demographics of Illinois'children regarding after -school programs. First, it should be noted that despite large variations in youth numbers (Cook County vs. Brown County), youth between the ages of 6 and 17 years comprise approximately 18% of Illinois'total population. Comparing 1990 and 2000 census data shows that medium-sized communities (50,000 to 150,000) are growing the fastest, while rural communities are slowly decreasing. Chicago remains stable.

Figure 5 shows that using the universal approach for after-school programs for children ages 6 to17 would mean providing services to nearly 2.2 million Illinois youth. A more targeted approach would be to identify disadvantaged populations based on the number of families and children considered to be at high-risk or living in high-risk environments. That is, research strongly supports the reality that poor families, single-parent family structures, and disorganized communities have negative impacts on children and youth (Samampote, Bassett and Winsler, 2004). After-school programs provide an extraordinary opportunity to positively influence and support these children and families.

Figure 5. Estimates for After-School Services by Data Source

Needs Estimator	Estimated youth pop. 6-17 needing after-school services	State avg. and ranges for Illinois counties and 77 Chicago neighborhoods
Universal (all children 6-17) (Census, 2000)	2,184,305	State average: 18% Range: 6% to 32%
Youth in household with single working parent	437,167	State average: 17% Range: 6% to 46%
Youth in household with single parent in poverty	190,778	State average: 11% Range: 2% to 67%
Latchkey status (> 10 hrs. per wk) (IYS, 2002)	55,338 (8th grade only)	State estimate: 41% of 8th grade population
School failure (% not meeting Illinois Learning Standards and Academic Warning List (ISBE, 2002)	303,318 (not meeting ISBE standards)	State average: 38% (3rd, 5th and 8th grades only) Range: 19% to 80%

The Census data show that approximately 11% of Illinois single parents are in poverty, and 17% of single parents are working. Both populations are very likely to require after-school services, which total over 600,000 youth statewide.

From an educational perspective, it could be argued that all students not meeting the Illinois state achievement standards should enroll in after-school programs to improve their test scores. Using those criteria, approximately 38% of Illinois students (more than 300,000 children) are not meeting minimal academic standards. Illinois 21st Century Learning Community Centers provide services only to a small percentage of those children who are not meeting state standards.

Last, self- report (IYS) survey data with weighted estimates for the state found approximately 41% of 8th grade youth home alone for more than 10 hours per week. We have proposed a 10 hours per week home-alone threshold for risk among school age youth up to 8th grades. Although the survey estimate is limited to 8th grade students, it does suggest that over 50,000 eighth graders could use after-school programs and services, and this number would be substantially greater if children in the other grades were included.

There are several ways to estimate the need in Illinois for after-school programs and services using secondary data sources. The approach and priorities for determining need largely depend on whether policymakers and funders view needs based on a universal population, targeted populations, or educational criteria. It is apparent that after-school needs in Illinois are enormous compared with the existing resources, no matter which approach is used to estimate need. Further investigation of what after-school programs are available and some level of quality is urgently needed. Furthermore, this question of quality also is highly salient. Simply keeping children off the streets may not be optimal, as after-school programs that engage children and sustain their involvement to have a positive impact require high quality programming. Without question, single-parent families, poor families, students failing in schools, and students with working parents should be the primary targets for Illinois after-school programs and services, if they are to provide the best financial and human return. Only then will Illinois' disadvantaged children and families have the opportunities and supports necessary for achieving a promising future.

References

Battistich, V., E. Schaps, and N. Wilson. 2004. "Effect of Elementary School Intervention on Students 'Connectedness'to School and Social Adjustment During Middle School." *Journal of Primary Prevention* 24:243-262.

Belle, D. 1999. *The After-School Lives of Children: Alone with Others While Parents Work*. Mahwah, NJ: Erlbaum Publishers.

Carnegie Council on Adolescent Development 1989. *Turning Points: Preparing American Youth for the 21st Century*. Carnegie Corporation of New York, Washington, D.C

Hawkins, J. D., R.F. Catalano., and J.Y. Miller. 1992. "Risk and Protective Factors for Alcohol and Other Drug Problems in Adolescence and Early Adulthood: Implications for Substance Abuse Prevention." *Psychological Bulletin, 112:* 64-105.

Jessor, R, and S. Jessor. 1974. *Problem Behavior and Psychosocial Development: A Longitudinal Study Of Youth*. New York: Academic Press.

Mahoney, J.L., H. Lord, and E. Carryl. 2005. "An Ecological Analysis of After-School Participation and Development of Academic Performance and Motivational Attributes of Disadvantaged Children." *Child Development* 76:11-825

Markwood, A., M. McDermeit, and M. Godley. 2001. *Youth Study On Substance Use: Comparing The 1995, 1997, 1998 And 2000 Results*. (Report to the Illinois Department of Human Services). Bloomington, IL: Chestnut Health Systems.

Mulhall, P., D. Stone, and B. Stone. 1996. "Home Alone: Is It A Risk Factor For Middle School Youth Drug Use?" *Journal of Drug Education* 26:37-46.

National Assessment of Educational Progress. 1998. *School Poverty and Academic Performance: NAEP Achievement in High-Poverty Schools - A Special Evaluation Report for the National Assessment of Title I*. Retrieved August 17, 2002 from http://www.ed.gov/pubs/school-poverty.

National Governors Association. 1998. *Preparing Youth for the Workforce under Welfare Reform*. Center for Best Practices-Employment and Social Services Policies Studies Division. July, 8-9.

Newman, S.,A., Fox, J.A., Flynn, E.A. and Christeson, W. 2000. *America's After-School Choice: The Prime Time For Juvenile Crimes, Or Youth Enrichment And Achievement. A Report from Fight Crime: Invest in Kids*. Washington, DC: Fight Crime: Invest in Kids.

Resnick, M D., P.S Bearman, R. W. Blum, K. E.Bauman, and K. M, Harris. 1997. "Protecting Adolescents from Harm." *Journal of the American Medical Association 278*:823-632.

Richardson, J., B. Radziszewska, C. Dent, and B.R. Flay. 1993. "Relationship Between After-School Care of Adolescents and Substance Abuse Risk Taking, Depressed Mood, and Academic Achievement." *Pediatrics* 92:32-38.

Riley, D. 1997. "Using Local Research to Change 100 Communities for Children and Families." *American Psychologist* 52:424-433.

Sarampote, N.C., Bassett, and A. Winsler. 2004. "After-School Care: Child Outcomes and Recommendations for Research and Policy." *Child and Youth Care Forum*, 44, (5) 329-348.

U.S. Department of Education, 2003. *When Schools Stay Open Late: The National Evaluation Of The 21st Century Learning Centers Programs: First Year Findings*. Office of the Secretary, Washington, DC

Note

*This work was supported, in part, by a grant from the Illinois Department of Human Services and Illinois State Board of Education under the Illinois After-School Partnership Initiative.

Chapter 9

*Effectiveness of the Conservation Reserve Enhancement Program in Illinois**

Madhu Khanna

The Conservation Reserve Program (CRP) was established in 1985 to promote crop land retirement to reduce environmental damages from agricultural production. Initially designed as a soil protection program, the CRP has evolved into a multi-objective program for reducing off-site impacts of sediment and chemical run-off on water quality, enhancing wildlife habitat, and improving air quality. In 1996, Congress authorized the creation of subprograms within CRP to more cost-effectively target high-priority, environmentally sensitive land in designated geographic areas not being offered for enrollment through CRP. This led to the creation of the continuous CRP and its variant, the Conservation Reserve Enhancement Program (CREP). Land selected for enrollment in CRP for a 15 year period can be enrolled in a CREP contract for an extended period of 15 or 35 years or permanently. Unlike the CRP, the CREP seeks to achieve numerically defined environmental goals in critically important areas within states. As of 2003, there were 26 CREP agreements in 24 states amounting to 1.4 million acres (USDA, 2003a).

The CREP in Illinois, established in March 1998, targets environmentally sensitive crop land in the Illinois River basin. It is being implemented through a federal-state-local partnership with the state of Illinois providing 20% of the total program costs. The goals for Illinois CREP include a 20% reduction in off-site sediment loadings, a 10% reduction in nutrient loadings, a 15% increase in populations of waterfowl and state and federally listed species, and a 10% increase in native fish and mussel stocks in the lower reaches of the Illinois River. The program was successful in meeting its acreage enrollment goal. The total discounted costs of the Illinois CREP since its inception are approximately $228 million of which $50 million have been contributed by the state[1]. Recently, Illinois has committed to provide another $10 million to enroll more land in the CREP. This will leverage $40 million from the U. S. Department of Agriculture for CREP enrollments.

Public agencies have to tackle several important issues in designing the CREP. These include (a) defining the eligibility criteria for land that can be enrolled in the program, (b) identifying the mechanism to be used for selecting land to be enrolled, (c) establishing a schedule of monetary incentives so that landowners are willing to voluntarily retire land from crop production and (d) deciding on the criteria for distributing the CREP enrollments and contribution to CREP goals across different watersheds within the eligible region. This chapter discusses the economic issues underlying the design and implementation of the CREP, evaluates the performance of CREP enrollments in two watersheds in Illinois (La Moine watershed and Lower Sangamon watershed) and concludes with some policy alternatives for design of the CREP in the future.

Implementation of Illinois CREP

Illinois has the largest CREP in the country with 132,000 acres enrolled between March 1998 and October 2001. This section describes how the program is implemented.

Eligibility Criteria

Illinois CREP focuses on enrolling land in the floodplain of the Illinois River Basin. Eligible land must be located either in the 100-year floodplains, on wetlands, or on sloping land (erosion index of 12 or more) adjacent to established riparian buffers.[2] The program currently seeks to select 85% of the land from the 100-year floodplains and 15% from the erodible lands next to a riparian buffer. Even within this narrowly defined eligible land area there is considerable variation among land parcels in terms

128

of their sediment generation potential, contribution to wildlife habitat and other environmental benefits. These differences arise due to differences in land quality, topography, location relative to water bodies, and management practices. There is also variation in the economic costs of enrolling land, measured by the fore-gone profits from crop production. With the above definition of eligible land there would be over five million crop land acres eligible for enrollment in Illinois CREP. There was, thus, a need and a potential for selectivity in enrolling the 132,000 acres in the program.

Selection Criteria

Illinois CREP considered all crop land offered for enrollment from the eligible area as being alike and enrolled it in the order in which applications were made. Producers had to be willing to apply one or more of the approved conservation practices such as riparian buffer and wildlife habitat and were then automatically accepted at the maximum soil rental rate on a first-come basis. This selection criterion is very different from that used by the CRP. The CRP relies on an Environmental Benefits Index (EBI) for selecting land parcels for enrollment during specific sign-up periods[3]. Parcels are ranked on the basis of the EBI and those with the highest EBIs are enrolled until acreage limits are met. The use of the EBI enables competitiveness in the selection process and allows inclusion of multiple environmental benefits and increases the cost effectiveness of the program. In contrast, producers can submit applications for enrollment in the CREP throughout the year, thus sidestepping CRP signups, the EBI and competitive bidding. The EBI is not used for selecting CREP enrollments because the EBI was not designed to be applied at the small landscape scale at which the CREP operates. It is believed that with the joint restriction of eligible area and conservation practices all land considered eligible for the CREP would generate EBI scores above the typical cutoff level used in the CRP.

Rental Payments

The CREP is a voluntary program, where landowners choose to offer their land for enrollment in return for a rental payment. Compensation to land owners is based on quality of soil of the land enrolled. All enrollees receive the maximum soil rental rates for their soil type. In addition, incentives and bonus payments are made to encourage highly erodible land and land in riparian buffers and there is 50% cost-sharing of establishment costs. These generous rental payments were considered necessary for attracting environmentally sensitive but expensive crop land that is not being enrolled in the CRP. The acreage offered by landowners for enrollment in the CREP was much larger than the acreage goal of the program and by October 2001 there was a waiting list of landowners wanting to enroll in the CREP. While this rental payment scheme made the CREP easy to implement, it resulted in much higher costs of the program both compared to the CRP and compared to alternative approaches to providing incentives for CREP enrolments (as discussed below). In contrast to the CREP, the CRP awards points for offering land at rental rates below the maximum soil rental rates, thus fostering competitiveness and incentives for lowering the costs of the program. While CRP rental rates in Illinois are $80 per acre on average, those for CREP are almost twice as high (USDA, FSA 2005).

Distribution of Enrollments across Watersheds

By enrolling land on a first-come basis, program administrators assumed that all watersheds were alike in their costs and benefits of achieving the environmental goals of CREP. There were no explicit criteria for distributing land enrollments or contribution to environmental goals across watersheds. Instead of this approach, land enrollments could have been distributed across the eligible region in several alternative ways. The total acreage to be enrolled could be uniformly divided across the eligible watersheds. Alternatively, each watershed could be allocated enrollments such that it meets the environmental goals of the program. For example, each watershed could enroll acreage such that it can individually meet the 20% off-site sediment abatement goal. A third approach would be to allocate enrollments such that they meet the environmental goals in the aggregate, that is, the 132,000 acres collectively reduce sediment loadings by 20%. The approach selected can have significant effects on the effectiveness of the program.

130

Performance of CREP Enrollments

We studied the performance of the land parcels enrolled in the CREP in two watersheds in Illinois in terms of their contribution to reducing off-site sediment loadings in waterbodies and the costs of retiring them from crop production. In the Lower Sangamon Watershed 3,608 acres of land, representing 5% of its cropland are enrolled in the CREP while in the La Moine Watershed 5,889 acres representing 16% of its cropland are enrolled. In both watersheds the majority of the CREP enrollments are in the 100-year floodplains of the Illinois River.

We used detailed data from publicly available Geographic Information System (GIS) databases to obtain elevation, location of streams, watershed boundary and soil characteristics at a 300 feet by 300 feet resolution for each of these watersheds. We estimated off-site sediment abatement that would be achieved during a five-year storm event by retiring an eligible parcel using a hydrological model. We also estimated the economic costs of retiring a land parcel from crop production, measured by the profits from crop production. For some watersheds, we used soil specific rental rates used by program administrators (for details see Khanna et al., 2003).

According to our calculations, retiring the 3,608 acres that are enrolled in the CREP in the Lower Sangamon Watershed reduced sediment loadings by 12%, from 38,642 tons to 33,966 tons. We also estimated that the average cost was $126 per ton of sediment abatement and $163 per acre of retired land. In the La Moine Watershed we found that CREP enrollments abated sediment loadings by 23% from 28,644 tons to 21,799 tons at an average cost of $90 per ton of sediment abatement and $99 per acre of land enrolled in the program. The CREP does, therefore, appear to have been effective in reducing sediment loadings into the Illinois River, although the extent to which it has done so, varies across watersheds (see Yang, Khanna, Farnsworth and Onal, 2005; Yang, Khanna, Farnsworth, 2005).

Alternative Approaches to CREP Implementation

We next examined the effectiveness of other decision rules for eligibility, selection and rental payments for meeting program objectives of sediment abatement. Some of the key findings of that research are presented here.

Eligibility Criteria

The CREP was originally conceived of as a buffer program but it evolved into a program that focused on enrolling land in the floodplains. It, therefore, excluded land in the riparian buffer that was not in the floodplain but could have highly erodible soil. Moreover, in areas where the floodplains were very wide, land that was relatively distant from waterbodies was also eligible for enrollment. A more stringent definition of eligibility of land for enrollment in the CREP would have been more effective. In our study, we defined the eligible region as the land within a 900-foot buffer along all streams and tributaries of the Illinois River. All land eligible under this definition is not within riparian areas (that is the 100-year floodplain) considered to be eligible for enrollment in the CREP. For small streams in the Illinois River Basin, the 900-foot buffer generally exceeds the 100-year floodplain boundaries, while for major tributaries and for Illinois River, this buffer could be narrower than the floodplain. This definition allows any sloping cropland adjacent to a stream or a riparian buffer within 900 feet of a stream to be eligible for enrollment in the CREP even though it may not be in the floodplain. As discussed below, our analysis shows that cost-effectiveness can be achieved by selecting only those land parcels within 300-600 feet of a water body. Restricting eligibility to a narrow buffer would facilitate greater cost-effectiveness in meeting program goals. It would prevent land parcels that are further away from a waterbody and, therefore, contributing less to sediment loadings from enrolling in CREP.

Selection Criteria

In both watersheds, we found that while the economic costs of enrolling land do not vary much across eligible land parcels, the potential contribution of parcels to off-site sediment abatement varies a great deal. The contribution of a parcel to sediment loadings in a waterbody depends on the volume of sediment generated on a parcel (which consists of the amount of sediment run-off generated by that parcel as well as the amount of sediment run-off flowing in from upland parcels) and the potential of downslope land parcels to trap that sediment run-off. The contribution of a parcel to off-site sediment loadings is higher if the parcel has highly erodible soil quality, a high slope and if it is closer to a waterbody. This contribution would also depend on management practices of that parcel. Land parcels are typically heterogeneous in their contribution to off-site sediment loadings. Similarly, they differ in their costs of retiring from crop production because profits per acre vary depending on soil quality, management practices and other production decisions. As a result the ratio of off-site abatement benefits to cost of enrolling varies a great deal across the eligible parcels.

We ranked eligible parcels on the basis of their benefits to cost ratio in the Lower Sangamon Watershed and selected the top ranking parcels until the 12% level of abatement being achieved currently by the CREP was realized. We found that this level of abatement could be achieved at a much lower average cost of $31 per ton instead of $126 per ton of abatement and with an enrollment of less than a third of the acres currently enrolled in the program. In the La Moine Watershed, we selected the same number of acres as currently enrolled in the CREP in that watershed after ranking parcels according to their abatement benefits to cost ratio. We found that selecting parcels on this basis could lower the per-ton abatement cost to $40 per ton instead of the currently realized cost of $90 per ton. It would also increase the amount of sediment abated to 45% instead of 23% of the pre-program level.

The current approach used by the CREP for selecting the parcels to be enrolled in the program has resulted in high costs, in part because a large proportion of the land currently enrolled in the program is in the flat floodplains and almost a fourth of the acres are more than 900 feet from a water body. The current method for land enrollment also does not ensure that the land enrolled in the program will be able to meet the environmental goals of the program. This land is less erosive and traps less sediment from inland areas of the watershed while being more productive and costly to retire. Instead, to achieve the abatement goals of the program cost-effectively, we should focus more on enrolling land parcels that are highly sloping, closer to a water body, that receive larger upland sediment inflow, generate more on-site erosion and have lower profits per acre.

Since estimation of the sediment abatement benefit from retiring a parcel is complicated, data intensive and requires technical expertise, we developed a simplified method to do so (for details see Yang, Khanna, Farnsworth and Onal, 2005; Yang, Khanna, Farnsworth, 2005). The sediment abatement potential of a land parcel can be predicted on the basis of observable characteristics of the parcel (such as its soil erodibility, its distance from the nearest waterbody, and its slope) using information that is likely to be easily available with agencies that administer conservation programs such as the National Resource Conservation Service. Using these predicted benefits and selecting the parcels with highest benefits to cost ratio we found that we could very closely approximate the pattern of land retirement that would be achieved using more accurate estimates of the contribution of each parcel to sediment abatement benefits.

Rental Payments

The CREP is an incentive-based program where landowners enroll their land if program payments exceed the returns from crop production. The program currently pays rental rates based on soil types only, irrespective of location and slope of land which can influence their environmental benefits from land retirement. Instead, incentives for retiring land parcels that could contribute the most to sediment abatement and whose opportunity costs are low could be created through a variable rental payment scheme based on benefit to cost ratios of parcels. For example, rental rates offered to parcels could increase as the distance of the parcel from a water body decreases, as slope of the parcel increases and its soil erodibility increases. These rental payments could also be lower for parcels that have very high opportunity costs of retiring, in order to encourage the lower cost parcels to enroll in the CREP. Using a rule similar to that used to predict the sediment abatement potential of each eligible parcel to determine rental rates that should be offered to each parcel, we find that by offering parcel-specific rental rates we can significantly lower costs of enrollment per acre while increasing the amount of sediment abatement achieved per acre (for details see Yang,

134

Khanna, Farnsworth, 2005).

Even though a simple rule for determining parcel-specific rate in each watershed could be devised, it would impose an informational and computational burden on program administrators. An alternative, simpler approach would be to place a maximum cap on rental rate per acre to be paid in a watershed. We find that even this would be more effective than the current approach of offering the maximum cash rental rates to all parcels. In the Lower Sangamon Watershed, a rental cap policy would result in an average abatement cost of $49 per ton, which is substantially less than the current estimated cost of the CREP ($126 per ton), but $18 per ton more than the parcel-specific rental rate policy. The enrollment pattern achieved by the rental cap instrument was similar to that achieved by the parcel specific policy. However, unlike the parcel-specific rental rate policy, a relatively large proportion of the targeted land under the rental cap policy was more than 600 feet away from water bodies. While this instrument would create incentives for sloping land that is generally less productive and more erosive than the floodplain land, and thus has lower costs to enroll, it would not attract some critical land parcels that contribute most to off-site sediment loading.

Distribution of Enrollments across Watersheds

We examined the cost-effectiveness of two alternative approaches for distributing enrollments across twelve contiguous watersheds in Illinois' designated CREP region (Yang, Khanna, Farnsworth and Onal, 2003). This area lies within the boundaries of Brown, Cass, Mason, Menard, Morgan, and Sangamon counties in Illinois. Land enrollments could be distributed either such that each watershed achieves 20% sediment abatement or such that the twelve watersheds achieve 20% sediment abatement in the aggregate, with some watersheds abating more and others abating less than 20%. We find the latter approach is significantly more cost-effective (costing $39 per ton of sediment abatement as compared to $48 per ton under the former), because it allows those watershed where the benefits of abatement are high and the costs of abatement are low to enroll more land in CREP as compared to other watersheds. This outcome, however, cannot be achieved by enrolling land on a first-come basis, Instead, land parcels should be ranked on the basis of their costs and benefits both within and across watersheds and selected such that the cost of the last ton of sediment abated by each watershed is the same. Given the heterogeneity in benefits and costs across watersheds in the eligible region, enrolling the same number of acres in each watershed would not be a cost-effective way to achieve the 20% sediment abatement goal of CREP. Watersheds with a larger proportion of crop land that has a higher slope and more erodible soils and that is less productive should enroll more land in CREP than other watersheds.

Conclusions and Policy Implications

In contrast to the CRP, the CREP was established to achieve numerically defined environmental benefits by restricting definition of the eligible region for the program. However, it lacks any mechanism for enrolling eligible land in a selective manner to ensure that land parcels with higher environmental benefit to opportunity cost ratios would be enrolled in the program or that program goals will be achieved. Parcels are enrolled using a queue system based on the time of application to the program. Our analysis shows that geographical limitations on eligibility, without any competitive mechanism for selecting land parcels, do not guarantee cost-effectiveness of a land retirement program.

Illinois CREP does, however, offer the potential to be more cost-effective if it could target land parcels that are closer to a water body, highly sloping and have highly erodible land quality. As Illinois prepares for fresh enrollment in the CREP with new federal and state investment of $50 million, it could make policy modifications to increase cost-effectiveness of the program. First, its eligible region should be limited to a narrow buffer, with a width of about 900 feet, along all streams and tributaries of the Illinois River Basin and not be restricted to the 100-year floodplain. Furthermore, there is a need to design a selection mechanism to choose among land parcels offered for enrollment in the CREP. Second, modifications in certain program criteria are also desirable. For example, the program currently seeks to select 85% of land from the 100-year floodplains and only 15% from the erodible lands next to a riparian buffer. Since sloping land contributes more to sediment erosion and is also less productive, and thus cheaper to retire, it would be preferable to modify the eligibility criteria to include all cropland in the riparian buffer. Third, supplementing this modified eligibility criteria with a rental payment instrument that varies rents based on observable site-specific characteristics, more precise targeting could be achieved to closely replicate the cost-effective land enrollment pattern. Observable characteristics, such as on-site erodibility, soil productivity and distance from a waterbody, can play an important role in determining rental payments to target cost-effective enrollment. Our analysis shows that even a simplified tool for estimating sediment abatement benefits based on observable land characteristics can be effective in achieving 95% of the benefits that would be obtained using the estimate of potential benefits provided by a complicated hydrologic model. In summary, a competitive selection process that takes environmental benefits and rental costs into consideration before enrolling parcels can improve performance of the CREP in Illinois relative to current levels achieved by enrolling parcels on a first-come first-enrolled basis. These findings are significant in a setting where farmers make voluntary decisions in response to incentive payments and scarcity of funding for environmental protection becomes more restrictive for program administrators. Finally, it is important to define criteria for distributing land enrollments across different watersheds within the eligible region.

Our analysis, however, focused only on the sediment abatement objective of the CREP. The wildlife habitat or wetland preservation benefits provided by existing enrollments that are in the floodplain are not being considered here. Incorporating those environmental considerations would make estimation of environmental benefits more complicated but would not change the two main arguments of this chapter. First, there is need to design a mechanism to select the parcels for enrollment in the program in order to achieve program goals cost-effectively. Second, incentives need to be created through a variable rental payment policy to target those land parcels that could contribute most effectively to achievement of the goals of the program.

References

Khanna, M., W. Yang, R. Farnsworth, and H. Onal. 2003. "Cost Effective Targeting of CREP to Improve Water Quality with Endogenous Sediment Deposition Coefficients." *American Journal of Agricultural Economics* 85(3): 538-553.

Yang, W., M. Khanna, R. Farnsworth, and H. Onal. 2003. "Integrating Economic, Environmental and GIS Modeling to Determine Cost Effective Land Retirement in Multiple Watersheds." *Ecological Economics* 46: 249-267.

Yang, W., M. Khanna, R. Farnsworth, and H. Onal. 2005. "Is Geographical Targeting Cost-Effective? The Case of the Conservation Reserve Enhancement Program in Illinois." *Review of Agricultural Economics* 27(1): 70-88, 2005.

Yang, W., M. Khanna, R. Farnsworth, and H. Onal . 2005 "Effectiveness of Conservation Programs in Illinois and Gains from Targeting,"*American Journal of Agricultural Economics*, December, 2005 (forthcoming).

USDA, FSA. 2003b. *Conservation Reserve Program: Final Programmatic Environmental Impact Statement.* January (http://www.fsa.usda.gov/-dafp/cepd/epb/impact.htm#final). Accessed November 17, 2003.

USDA, FSA. 2005. Conservation Reserve Program, Monthly Summary - March 2005. Accessed on May 6, 2005 (http://www.fsa.usda.-gov/dafp/cepd/stats/Mar2005.pdf).

Notes

[*]Funding for this research from the Illinois Council for Food and Agricultural Research is gratefully acknowledged. The contributions of my collaborators Wanhong Yang, Richard Farnsworth and Hayri Onal to the research on which this chapter is based is also acknowledged.

[1] http://www.ilcrep.org/.

[2] Additionally, land eligible for enrollment in CREP must have been owned or operated by a producer for a minimum of 12 months and planted an agricultural

commodity at least four of the previous six years. This eligibility criteria is similar to that of the CRP.

[3] During specific sign-up periods land parcels offered for enrollment are awarded points based on their location in state or national conservation priority areas and the impact on surface and ground water quality, erosion reduction, wildlife cover, and air quality. A weighted summation of these points is used to obtain an EBI for each parcel.

Chapter 10

Political Corruption and Ethics Policy in Illinois[*]

Kent Redfield

It is ironic that the two individuals who have come to symbolize the corruption of Illinois politics were never indicted for political corruption. Richard J. Daley, the late Mayor of Chicago, presided over the greatest urban political machine of the second half of the 20th century. Hundreds of public officials and public employees that were part of that machine went to jail in the 1960s and 1970s. But it is unlikely that Richard J. Daley's sudden death in 1975 cheated any grand jury investigation. All of Daley's biographers agree that his political life was motivated by power, not private gain. In a political culture like Illinois that honors power and tolerates corruption, an overly greedy, corrupt politician is a much more inviting target for law enforcement than a politician who is merely corrupt. The other Illinois icon of political corruption is Paul Powell. It has been more that 35 years since the death of Illinois Secretary of State Paul Powell and the subsequent discovery of more than $800,000 in cash in his Springfield hotel room, some of it stored in shoe boxes. Yet the shoe box remains one of the most enduring images of political corruption in Illinois. Powell was the "grey fox of Vienna," three -time Speaker of the Illinois House and deal-maker extraordinaire. He never made more than $30,000 a year from elected office; yet his estate, including the $800,000 in cash, was valued at more than $2.6 million. A significant portion of Powell's money undoubtedly came from the Illinois horse racing interests. Illinois Governor Otto Kerner's 1972 federal income tax evasion conviction focused how he obtained stock in horse racing tracks and whether his official actions increased the value of his stock. If Powell had not died in 1970, we can only speculate whether then U.S. Attorney, and future Illinois Governor, James R. Thompson, might have turned his attention to Powell after securing the conviction of Kerner.

It would be comforting to presume that Daley and Powell are ancient history, with little relevance to an analysis of ethics policy in Illinois. Hasn't a lot changed since the 1970s? In 1974 Illinois passed a campaign finance law requiring reporting and disclosure of contributions and expenditures. Illinois has an open meetings law, a freedom of information act, a procurement law setting out requirements for competitive bidding, and a law requiring elected officials and most public employees to file a statement of economic interests. Illinois' lobbyist registration and reporting law was significantly revised in 1994. Major changes in the campaign finance law and a gift ban law prohibiting public officials and employees from receiving things of value from those doing business with government were enacted in 1998. In spite of all these laws dealing with political ethics and public corruption, events since the spring of 2002 suggest that they are not working very well. The reality is that the political ethics of Daley and Powell are all too familiar to even a casual observer of politics as usual in Illinois.

Since the spring of 2002, we have seen the indictment and conviction of former Governor George Ryan's campaign fund (Citizens for Ryan) and Ryan's chief of staff when he was Secretary of State. These convictions were the result of an ongoing investigation into public corruption in the Secretary of State's office that has yielded 79 indictments and 73 convictions or guilty pleas. Former Governor Ryan went on trial in the fall of 2005, charged with multiple acts of political corruption. Another Federal investigation resulted in the indictment of a former Speaker of the Illinois House's chief of staff in the spring of 2005.

The years of 2004 and 2005 have also seen a steady series of press stories about patronage hiring in state government and about possible links between contracts awarded to companies and campaign contributions made to current Governor Rod Blagojevich's campaign fund. In September of 2005, the U.S. attorney's office made public two plea agreements from individuals charged in federal indictments with extorting money from firms seeking investment in Illinois state retirement funds. Those plea agreements contained hearsay testimony that linked the activities of those pleading guilty to close associates of the Governor, who strongly denied any knowledge or involvement.

In October of 2005 ongoing federal investigations into hiring practices in state agencies became public and were acknowledged by the Governor's office.

Not all the recent action on the public corruption front has been taking place at the state level. During 2005 alone, public officials in East St. Louis were convicted on charges of vote fraud. In Chicago a federal investigation into a scandal in a hired truck program has produced 36 indictments and 23 guilty pleas. Of even more importance, the hired truck scandal prompted an investigation into political hiring in the City of Chicago that has led all the way to the mayor's office. In August, Mayor Richard M. Daley was interviewed by federal prosecutors about the hiring practices of the city. With a number of indictments, guilty pleas and resignations, and an ongoing investigation, any claim that the old Chicago political machine had died appears premature.

How Corrupt Is Illinois Politics?

Political corruption falls into three broad areas of illegal or unethical activities. First, there is corruption that directly subverts the political process. Buying votes or intimidating specific groups of voters are examples. Second, there is corruption that results in public resources being used for political purposes. Examples are putting an unqualified political supporter on the public payroll or requiring public employees to do campaign work while on public time. Finally, there is corruption that results in public authority being used for private gain. Public officials extorting money or taking bribes from private firms seeking governmental contracts are examples of this type of corruption.

On all levels, Illinois has a long history of public corruption. In the last 50 years, we have had a Governor (Kerner), an Attorney General (Scott) and an Auditor of Public Accounts (Hodge) along with congressmen, legislators, judges, and local officials almost too numerous to count go prison for public corruption. The excesses of Chicago Mayor Richard J. Daley and Illinois Secretary of State Paul Powell have already been noted. Political scandals in Chicago and Cook County occur with such frequency that they require names (i.e., Gray Lord, Silver Shovel, and Hired Truck) just to keep them apart. The place of Illinois in the history of political patronage is very secure. The U.S. Supreme Court case declaring unconstitutional the practice of firing public employees because they supported the wrong political party bears the name of a Cook County Sheriff (Elrod). The case outlawing the use of political party affiliation as the primary factor in hiring public employees bears the name of an Illinois Governor (James R. Thompson). It is a tribute to the power of Illinois' political culture that the crusading U.S. Attorney who rode his reputation as a corruption fighter to election as Illinois Governor ended his four terms in office presiding over a patronage hiring system that would be declared unconstitutional by the U.S. Supreme Court. Any list of the most politically corrupt states in the nation has Illinois at or near the top, along with Louisiana and New Jersey.

The fruits of our recent politics stand out in stark terms in the federal indictments of Governor George Ryan, his campaign fund, and his former chief of staff. Hundreds of pages recount in great detail the abuses of public power and the betrayal of the public trust to benefit private interests and political ends. From major offenses such as diverting public employees to political campaigns and the fixing of government contracts and property leases to petty excesses such as stealing reams of paper, it is a picture of politics at its worst. For many Illinoisans, the charges and the sordid details only confirm their attitudes of total cynicism toward Illinois politics and government.

Why Is Illinois Politics So Corrupt?

What is the problem in Illinois? Do we just have a lot of bad people? Or do we have a political system that corrupts many of the people who get involved with politics? Or is it something in the water? The answer is all of the above. While not actually the water, the basic Illinois political culture that everyone in the state grows up with and experiences firsthand contributes to a climate of political corruption. Our political culture does little to attract good people to politics and even less to restrain the bad people who get into politics. And the political system we have developed in Illinois both reflects and reinforces the corruption of our political culture.

Commonly shared attitudes and beliefs about politics shape how we think about politics and what we expect from politics and our politicians. Illinois has a political culture that emphasizes power, winning, control, and jobs over the public interest or good public policy. Illinoisans tend to think of politics as primarily a business, a vocation that people take up in order to pursue personal interests. Not only are we taught at our dinner tables and in our classrooms and churches and by our news media that politics is a business, we also learn that it is a dirty business. The expectations are that politicians will cut corners in order to win and that they will place the interests of those who supported them above the interests of the general public. Politics is regarded as the province of professional politicians rather than concerned citizens. These kinds of attitudes translate into low expectations about politics along with a tolerance for corruption, a lack of incentives for citizens to participate in the process, and an acceptance of patronage as the driving force in public employment. Political scientists call this type of political culture "individualistic." Illinois has long been the poster boy for individualistic politics. Our expectations and our standards for politics are very, very low and then our politicians live up to them.

The political structures that have developed in Illinois and the type of politicians that have dominated Illinois since statehood tend to favor the interests of the politicians and private interests over the general interests of the public. Illinois election laws discourage easy access and widespread participation in the process. Access to public documents is limited and often discouraged by those in power. Public disclosure of the official actions of public officials is also limited. Disclosure of information about the private interests of public officials is limited in both content and access. There are no limits on how much a person, association, company, or union can contribute to a political candidate. Nor are there any prohibitions against campaign contributions from business and professional interests that are regulated by the state. Prohibitions against economic relationships between

144

public officials and private interests that might compromise public actions exist only in the broadest sense. In spite of laws and court rulings to the contrary, political patronage, rather than merit or need, dominates the staffing of state agencies.

Illinois political culture and the resulting political institutions do not encourage good people or people with talent to get involved with politics or to make state government a career. If anything, they discourage those people. At the same time the unscrupulous and the ambitious use the political system to pursue their individual goals while the weak are easily corrupted by the excesses.

What Are the Costs of Corruption?

There are costs to widespread public corruption in Illinois that go beyond the money spent on criminal investigations and trials. The first is a loss of legitimacy of the political process for the citizens of the state. Real corruption destroys public support for the political system. But the appearance of corruption is just as corrosive to the legitimacy of the political system as actual corruption. If everyone believes that Illinois politics is corrupt, then there is no reason to accept the policies or programs of government as having authority or to assume they have value. If everyone believes that all Illinois politicians are corrupt, or become corrupt soon after they take office, then there is no reason to support any attempts by political leaders to promote individual responsibility or collective obligations to solve the state's social pro blems or provide care for those in need.

The level of cynicism among Illinois citizens can be seen in a poll taken by the Survey Research Office at the University of Illinois at Springfield in early 2003. It found that more than three quarters of Illinois citizens believe that political corruption is widespread in state government. More than half thought political corruptions had gotten worse over the past eight years. More than 70% felt that law enforcement officials ignored allegations of political corruption.

The second cost is a loss of participation. Participation in politics is part of a civic culture that develops and ennobles both individuals and society. People are better and society is better when people participate in the political process. When citizens share in the decision making and have a vested interest in the outcomes, the foundations of the political system are strong. A corrupt political system does not encourage participation, nor does one where politics is reserved for the professional politician. When there is a widespread perception that politics is corrupt and someone else's business, the pool of citizens who participate and therefore make decisions and influence policy grows smaller. The state loses and individual citizens lose when a corrupt political system limits political participation.

The third cost is a weakening of the talent pool for public officials and those who work for government. A corrupt political system does not encourage young people to engage in politics or make politics a career. If there is a widespread perception that patronage hires and political interference make it difficult for talented people without political connections to get state jobs or to do a professional job of delivering services, then people will not become involved in government. The resulting talent pool of those who want to get involved with government as a career keeps shrinking.

The final cost is a deterioration of the quality of the public services that the state provides. Do-nothing state jobs, make-work contracts, and inflated, no-bid contracts take resources away from doing the real job of state government. A lack of good people and the diversion of public resources to political or private ends make it increasingly more difficult for the state to meet its basic obligations of providing for the education, health, and welfare of its citizens and protecting their environment. With an eye toward not doing anything that might upset the political dynamic that won the last election and a talent pool that is sorely lacking in innovative ideas, our politics also discourages the kinds of policy innovations and risk taking that leads to improved ways of addressing the state's obligations.

What Are the Solutions?

In response to the election of a new governor in 2002 and the continuing political scandals that dominated the attention of the news media, a new ethics law for pubic officials and public employees was passed during the fall 2003 veto session and signed into law. Among the most important parts of the law are the creation of ethics commissions for the executive and legislative branches and inspectors general to investigate complaints, requiring ethics training for state employees, placing new restrictions on gifts to public officials, prohibiting (for one year) state employees from taking jobs with companies with which they have been involved in negotiating large state contracts, and providing for increased access to lobbyist registration and economic interest statements.

In light of this most recent legislative success, do we really need more laws? And even more fundamentally, do laws really matter? Won't bad people do bad things in spite of the law? On one level, the problem is identifying the bad people and enforcing criminal laws. Stealing public funds, engaging in fraud, taking bribes and using public office to extort money has always been illegal. The most recent wave of indictments against Illinois public officials and public employees was not triggered by changes in state or federal law.

Having said all that, the fact still remains that laws do matter. A number of changes in the laws that govern Illinois politics would significantly reduce both actual corruption and the appearance of corruption. For example, look at something as simple as the gift ban law that was enacted in 1999. In Wisconsin, a lobbyist cannot buy so much as a cup of coffee for a legislator. There is a bright-line, zero-tolerance policy. The assumption is that just as there is no such thing as being a little bit pregnant, there is no such thing as being a little bit corrupt. The message of the Wisconsin public policy is clear. By contrast, in Illinois, the original gift ban legislation had a blanket exemption for "food and beverages consumed on the premises." In plain language, lobbyists could spend an unlimited amount "wining and dining" legislators. A limit of $75 per day was added by the 2003 changes in the law. But the fact still remains that it is legal for a lobbyist to buy $75 of food and beverages for a legislator in a restaurant, but illegal for the lobbyist to buy the same food and beverages at a grocery store and drop it off at the legislator's home. The message the law sends to participants and to the general public about political ethics is far from clear.

There are actions beyond throwing the bad people in jail that would result in major improvements to the ethical climate in Illinois politics. In general, these involve hardening the target, making actions more transparent, and raising expectations. Hardening the target means making it more difficult to engage in political corruption. Transparency means making political actions and processes more open and accessible so that corruption or the appearance of corruption becomes more visible. Raising expectations means convincing the public and politicians that standards of ethics need to be higher in politics than in any other sphere of human activity because politics, ultimately, is about the public's business.

We need to place limits and prohibitions on the role of money in Illinois politics. These changes would make engaging in corrupt activity more difficult. The Illinois campaign finance system is among the most wide-open, unrestricted system in the nation. Any group, any company, any union, any association, and any individual can contribute as much as they want whenever they want. The result is that companies seeking state contracts and companies with state contracts routinely make large ($25,000, $50,000, and $100,000) contributions to the campaign funds of those holding or seeking statewide legislative or local office. The same is true of labor unions, professional and trade associations, and companies seeking changes in Illinois law. When a large contributor is successful in obtaining a contract or a favorable change in the law, the losing side and the news media routinely draw the conclusion that the result indicates a *quid pro quo* or a conflict of interest. If true, the political process has been corrupted by money. If the linkage is credible, but ultimately untrue, the damage to the legitimacy of the process has already been done by allowing the perception of a conflict to exist in the first place. It is fine to say that most politicians are honest and that no one is selling a vote or a contract for $25,000. It is true that most people do not rob banks. But we do not test their resolve by leaving unattended stacks of $100 bills by the teller windows. Limiting contributions to a reasonable amount, such as $2,500 per election, would eliminate both the temptation for real corruption and the appearance of corruption.

The same case can be made for allowing only individuals to make contributions to political campaigns. Illinois is one of the few states with no prohibitions on who can contribute to campaigns. Corporations, labor unions, or associations as corporate entities cannot contribute directly to federal candidates. The principle that only people vote and so only people can contribute to political campaigns has existed at the federal level for more than fifty years. But even if the philosophical argument were not so compelling, the practical impact on corruption and the appearance of corruption from adopting prohibitions makes the change well worth doing. If companies seeking state contracts cannot contribute to public officials and if public officials cannot solicit companies that want or have state contracts, then both the appearance of *quid pro quos* and actual *quid pro quos* will no longer exist. The same logic applies to prohibitions on contributions from labor unions, corporations, or associations seeking changes in Illinois law. Individuals could still make contributions, but contribution limits and individual, rather than collective, responsibility for illegal actions would reduce the temptations and opportunities for individuals and public officials to engage in corrupt activities.

We need to dramatically increase the amount of information we have about public transactions and the private interests of public officials and public employees. We need to dramatically improve public access to the information that is available. The resulting focus would reveal conflicts of interests in the legislative and executive processes and make corruption and the appearance of corruption more visible and therefore less likely. Currently public employees and officials in Illinois file statements of economic interest with the Illinois Secretary of State. Lobbyists are required to register with the Secretary of State and file expenditure reports. All contracts between state government and private entities and all property leases between private entities and the state are filed with the Comptroller's office. The amount of information we have and the detail could be expanded. The open meetings act could be more completely understood and more uniformly enforced. The same is true for the freedom of information act.

But while more information is needed, there is an even stronger need to integrate information and provide timely and complete access. Once-a-year reports, paper reports, and reports posted online as PDF files are certainly better than not having reports or access to them. Having information in a number of databases is better than not having information in a database at all. But given the current state of electronic documents and database software, requiring electronic filing and semi-annual updates for statements of economic interests and lobbyist registration is not unreasonable. The same is true for requiring comprehensive campaign disclosure reports to be filed every three months rather than every six months. All of this information should be accessible online in searchable databases. The next step would be to bring all of the information about economic interests, lobbying activities and registration, campaign contributions and expenditures, and state contracts and property leases together in one integrated database that is searchable online. The goal would be to enter a name of an individual or a company and search all of the data available for relationships with public officials, public employees, and state agencies. Reporting and disclosure cast sunshine on the political process. In some cases it exposes real or potential conflicts of interest. In others it provides verification that no conflicts exist. Just as important, the fear of disclosure discourages actions and relationships that cannot stand the light of day.

We need to make the processes used to hire public employees and to award government contracts and property leases more merit based and more open to the public and the news media. This would both harden the target and increase transparency. Patronage in hiring and pin-striped patronage in awarding contracts and leases may not have been invented in Illinois government, but they survive and thrive here like few other places. We need laws, executive orders, and agency rules at all levels of government in Illinois that increase the talent pool for public employment and ensure that highly qualified people are hired to fill those jobs. We need to reduce the opportunity for corruption in public hiring by adopting measures that make information about job openings and hiring procedures public and accessible, provide greater specificity for job titles, and require more rigorous, differentiated testing. In the awarding of state contracts and property leases,

150

bans on political contributions from those having them or seeking to acquire them would be good. A complete ban on corporate contributions would be better. In addition we need greater restrictions on no-bid contracts, more competitive leasing processes, more disclosure by those seeking to do business with the state, greater authority for inspectors general, and greater disclosure and access to the public records of these transactions.

Finally, we need to raise public expectations about politics in order for Illinois politicians and citizens to reject the politics of personal and private interests and create a politics of the public interest and the common good. Changing Illinois' political culture has to start at the top. Elected officials at all levels of government have to take political ethics seriously and lead by example. Leading by example means that being a contributor, associate, or supporter of a public official is a disadvantage rather than an advantage when it comes to getting jobs, contracts, or political favors. Leading by example means that public employment is about bringing in the best and the brightest. Leading by example means providing high quality services and meeting the state's obligations rather than helping political supporters first and the public second. Each person in a position of public responsibility must consider what message is being sent to the citizens of the state by his or her decisions and actions.

Changing Illinois political culture also has to start at the bottom. Citizens have to expect more from their politicians and be willing to hold them accountable. One of the costs of public corruption has to be politicians paying a price at the polls for "business as usual" in Illinois. Convicting the bad guys and making it more difficult to engage in behavior that is corrupt or appears to be corrupt has to be done. It will reduce political corruption for a while. But long-term change in the nature of Illinois politics has to come from changes in the hearts and minds of Illinois citizens and Illinois politicians.

The Prospects for Ethics Reform in Illinois

How long will change take? Anyone working to bring ethics reform to Illinois politics soon learns that pessimism is often justified in the short run. But no one can look back over the last decade at the changes in Illinois laws and politics and not find reason for long-term optimism. The passage of the 2003 ethics bill shows that change is possible. The difficulty of achieving real change is aptly illustrated by implementation of part of that law. The 2003 ethics law required that all state employees receive annual ethics training. This could have taken the form of training workshops or interactive online instruction. When a branch of the military has a problem with its members complying with a policy, it is not uncommon for the entire organization to "stand down" from their normal activities while each unit spends a day carefully examining the policy and its application to the unit. These types of responses send a message that the organization takes the policy seriously and individuals will be held accountable. The annual ethics training program for all Illinois state employees consists of a short, online presentation of materials on workplace ethics followed by a ten-question, multiple-choice test. Each employee sits alone in front of a computer and goes through an exercise that would not challenge a sixth grader to pass it. Nor does it challenge anyone who takes it to think about the importance or application of ethics to their lives. The private responses of state employees to this training program are almost universal ridicule. Given an opportunity to send a message that political corruption is a serious problem and political ethics are important, the state has adopted a program that trivializes the issues and minimizes the importance. Adding insult to injury, the firm responsible for developing the online ethics training turned out to be a contributor to Governor Blagojevich's campaign fund. Fu ndamental change in Illinois political culture remains a work in progress.

Note

*Adapted from Kent Redfield, "Living Up to Low Standards: The Sad State of Political Ethics in Illinois," in the *Almanac of Illinois Politics: 2006* (*Illinois Issues* publications: forthcoming, 2006).

Chapter 11

Information Technology Gender Gap[*1]

Mo-Yin S. Tam and Gilbert W. Bassett, Jr.

Introduction

The issue of a gender gap has shifted from computer access and Internet connectivity to educational achievement and employment opportunities in information technology. The digital divide is more than just differences in connectivity; equalizing computer ownership and Internet access by itself does not necessarily translate into closing the opportunity gap created by the New economy. Despite the recent dot-com bust, individuals with technological skills and knowledge still command more rewarding economic opportunities. This is particularly the case for the high-IT core workforce where there have been the greatest increases in employment and highest increase in wages and salaries. This segment of the IT workforce includes computer programmers, computer scientists, computer engineers, and system analysts (with a college degree) whose jobs are directly involved in the "study, design, development, implementation, support or management of computer-based information systems, particularly software applications and computer hardware" (Craver, 1999). It is the gender gap in this sector of the IT workforce area that has increasingly received attention from government, researchers, and advocacy groups.

High-IT Core Workforce

The highest growth in employment has occurred in the high-IT core workforce. While employment in all IT occupations increased by 23% from 1992 to 1998 (double the increase in total U.S. nonfarm employment), employment in the high-IT core increased by 79%. Changes in other segments of the IT workforce were minimal.

With the surge in demand for IT workers, there has been a disproportionate increase in their wages, with the highest increase again occurring in the high-IT core sector. According to Sandra Cooke (2000), from 1992 to 1998, wages have been increasing at 5.8% per year for all workers in IT industries (compared to a 3.6% annual rate for the other private industry workers) while those in software and computer services industries, including computer programming services and software development, earned the highest average annual increase of 6.7%. In 1998, the average wage of all IT producing workers was $58,000 (85% higher than the $31,400 average wage for all private workers) while that for the high-IT core workers was $65,300. This represents a widening of the wage gap between the IT producing workers and all private workers by more than $10,000 between 1992 and 1998. A June 2001 poll of CIOs and HR managers of companies with sales $20 million or more reveals that the demand for IT workers remained strong with the number of unfilled IT positions having more than tripled since 1999. It was estimated that more than half of all jobs would require technological skills in the early 21st century.

Gender Gap in High-IT Core Workforce

Few women however are partaking in this technology boom. In 1997 women represented 46% of the total workforce, but only 25% of the professional IT workforce9 and 10% of the top IT jobs. While the gender gap in Internet usage has disappeared, the gender gap in female participation in the IT workforce persists.

Moreover, data in college enrollment suggests that this gap will widen since the number of IT majors has decreased in recent years. Recent NSF statistics show that the proportion of women receiving bachelor degrees in computer science actually dropped from 37% in 1984 to 28% in 1996. In 1998, only 22% of those seeking bachelor's degree in computer science were women and only 13% of the degrees in computer and electrical engineering were women. Moreover, the proportion of women with a master degree in computer science was even smaller with fewer still pursuing doctoral degrees.

The Economic Impact of the Technology Gender Gap

The gender gap in education achievement and employment opportunities places women at a significant disadvantage in a society that values computer technology. It drives a further income disparity between men and women. Weiner and Cain (1999) warned "if nothing is done, girls and women will be bystanders in the 21st century." This inequity has received increasing concern among researchers and women's interest groups. In addition, lack of women's participation means there are untapped resources that could fill the increasing demand for IT workers.

Understanding the Nature and Causes of the Technology Gender Gap

It is, therefore, important to understand the nature and causes of the gender gap in the high-IT core sector of the IT workforce. Thus, we use multi-year (1995-2000) student data from the University of Illinois at Chicago. Students who major in IT are those who will enter the high-IT core workforce upon graduation. To examine the nature and trend of IT majors and compare the extent of the IT major gender gap to that in science and engineering. Since in the last few years the gender gap in Internet usage has been apparently closing, we also consider how the IT-major gender gap has been changing. In addition, since it has been suggested that the technology gender gap may simply reflect ethnic and economic differences, we consider the gender gap within and across ethnic groups. We also analyze gender differences in the likelihood of becoming an IT major after controlling for math performance. We will see that that for similar math ability, women are far less likely to major in IT.

The Technology Gender Gap

The gender gap in college students majoring in information technology anticipates the gender gap in the high-IT core workforce. Graduates will enter the labor force as computer scientists, computer engineers, computer programmers, and system analysts.

The University of Illinois at Chicago is a comprehensive 4-year public university. Its undergraduate enrollment was almost constant from 1995 to 2000 with slightly more than 16,000 students. Consistent with general college enrollment, more than half of the undergraduate students are female. The proportion of female students has increased slightly from 52% in 1994 to 55% in 2000. The proportion of IT majors has almost doubled from 7% in 1995 to 13% in 2000.

Gender Gap in IT Majors

Table 1 shows the gender distribution of UIC undergraduate students in the various fields of science and technology in the fall semester of 2000.

Table 1: Percentage of Female Undergraduate Students in IT[a]
By Racial/ethnic Groups
Fall semester, 1994-2000, UIC

Year	Asian	Black	Hispanics	White	Total IT	Total U-Grad	IT Majors as a % of Entire Student Body
1995	22%	36%	24%	16%	21%	53%	7%
1996	23%	42%	23%	15%	21%	54%	8%
1997	26%	42%	27%	16%	23%	57%	9%
1998	30%	47%	30%	15%	26%	55%	12%
1999	29%	54%	35%	16%	27%	54%	13%
2000	30%	49%	29%	19%	27%	55%	13%

[a]Information technology (IT) includes majors in computer engineering, computer science, electrical engineering, management in information systems, and mathematics and computer science.

Women were underrepresented in all areas of science and engineering, except biological sciences. The percentage of women in the undergraduate student body was more than half (55%) while the percentages of women in physical sciences, engineering and IT are all less than 50%. In the case of IT majors, the percentage of women is only 27%.

Table 2 shows the gender gap indices for various fields of study. A gender gap index in a field of study denoted by $I_{field}^{(W)}$, indicates the number of times the number of women has to increase to eliminate the gender gap in that field.

156

**Table 2: Gender Gap Indices of Undergraduate Students
By Fields of Study, Fall Semester 2000, UIC**

	Engineering	IT	Physical Sciences	Entire Undergrad Student Body
$I_k^{(W)}$	3.8	3.3	1.4	1.0

The table shows a gender divide in all areas of physical sciences and technology with the highest gap in engineering and IT. Specifically, the number of women in IT has to be 3.3 times its current level to eliminate the gap.

Does the Gender Gap in IT Majors Reflect Ethnicity?

One possibility is that the overall gender gap simply reflects differences among ethnic groups. But as Table 3 shows, the gender gap exists within all ethnic groups. Hence, the gender gap reflects more than ethnic differences.

There are, however, considerable variations. Female underrepresentation is higher for Hispanics with a gender gap index of 3.3 compared to blacks (2.9) and Asians (2.5). A perhaps surprising result is that the gender gap is by far the highest among Whites (4.8). The number of white female students has to increase almost 5 times to eliminate the IT gender gap.

**Table 3: Gender Gap Indices in IT Areas By Racial/ethnic Groups
Fall semester, 1995-2000, UIC**

$I_{IT}^{j(W)}$	Asian	Black	Hispanics	White	Total	IT majors as a % of Entire Student Body
1995	3.4	3.7	4.1	5.4	4.2	7%
1996	3.2	3.4	4.4	6.0	4.3	8%
1997	2.8	3.4	3.8	5.7	3.8	9%
1998	2.3	3.1	3.2	6.3	3.4	12%
1999	2.5	2.9	2.8	5.7	3.4	13%
2000	2.5	2.9	3.3	4.8	3.3	13%

The Trend of the Gender Gap in IT Majors

What is the trend of the gap? Studies have shown that out-of-school activities affect career choice. In the 2000 issue of the "Falling Through the Net" series, it is shown that the gender gap of Internet usage has narrowed and in fact had disappeared by August 2000. But does the change in this out-of-school activity lead to a narrowing of the information technology gender gap?

Table 3 lists the gender gap indices in IT areas for UIC students from 1995 to 2000. The index is seen to decline from 4.2 in 1995 to 3.3 in 2000 for the entire student body, while the percentage of IT majors almost doubles from 7% in the fall of 1995 to 13% in the fall of 2000. Similar declines in the gap are evident for all ethnic groups. Hence, as the Internet usage gender gap has closed, the IT-major gender gap has narrowed, though it is still large in 2000. Further, the relative size of the gap among ethnic groups has remained constant throughout the period, with the largest gap among whites.

Technology Gender Gap and Math-Performance

Math performance is often cited as a major determinant for entry into science and technology. We consider the gender gap after taking into consideration differences in math performance by male and female students.

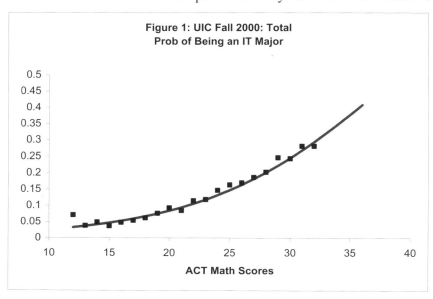

Figure 1: UIC Fall 2000: Total Prob of Being an IT Major

We use ACT math scores as an indicator of students' math performance. Using the fall 2000 student data at UIC, we construct the percentage of IT majors at each ACT score.

In our statistical analysis, we found that ACT score is a significant factor for IT participation. Figure 1 illustrates this relationship between ACT and IT participation. The curve closely follows the data.

Gender Gap in the Impact of Math Performance on the Odds of Being an IT Major

Is the math performance impact different between male and female students? Results from our analysis suggest that women are less likely to become an IT major even after we take into consideration the gender difference in math performance.

The gender gap is illustrated in Figure 2. The average ACT math scores for females (F) and males (M) are indicated on the horizontal axis of the figure. The probability of majoring in IT at various ACT scores is indicated on the vertical axis.

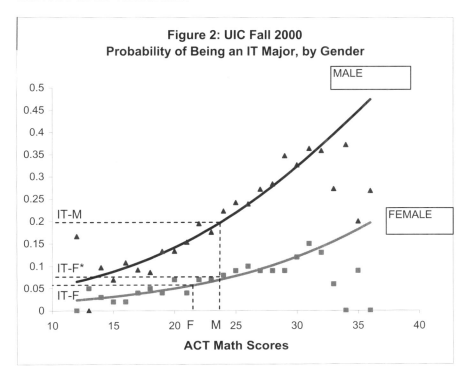

159

ACT math score is a significant factor in becoming an IT major for both groups. However, math performance is a much weaker factor for female students. A female student is less likely to become an IT major compared to a male student with the same ACT math score. Moreover, while the probability of a female student becoming an IT major increases with her ACT math score, the impact of ACT math scores is smaller for women than for men.

To see how much of the technology gender gap is due to the ACT math gender gap, consider the mean ACT scores for the female and male students. In the fall of 2000, the mean ACT score for the female students was 21.8 and that for male students was 23.9. As Figure 2 illustrates, the probability for a female student with a math ACT score of 21.8 to become an IT major is about 5%, denoted by IT-F in Figure 2. On the other hand, the probability for a male student with a math ACT score of 23.9 to become an IT major is 20%, denoted by IT-M in Figure 2. The technology gender gap is 15% (the difference between IT-M and IT-F illustrated in Figure 2).

How much of this gap is due to the gender math performance gap? Consider the situation where the gender math performance gap is closed. That is, suppose the mean math ACT score for female students were 23.9, the same as the mean ACT math score for male students. From the female curve in Figure 2, the probability for a female students with an ACT math score of 23.9 to become an IT major is 7%, denoted as IT-F* in Figure 2. Hence, a closing of the gender math performance gap would reduce—but far from eliminate—the technology gender gap. That is, it would become 13% instead of 15%, an absolute reduction of only 2%. Therefore, closing the math gender gap would eliminate less than 14% (i.e. 2/15) of the technology gender gap. Hence, while the gender gap would decrease with improving female math performance, its magnitude goes beyond math differences and evidently reflects other, perhaps social, reasons for majoring in IT.

The Trend of Gender Gap in the Impact of Math Performance

Has the math performance impact gender gap changed in the last few years? Figure 3 illustrates the trend from 1995 to 2000.

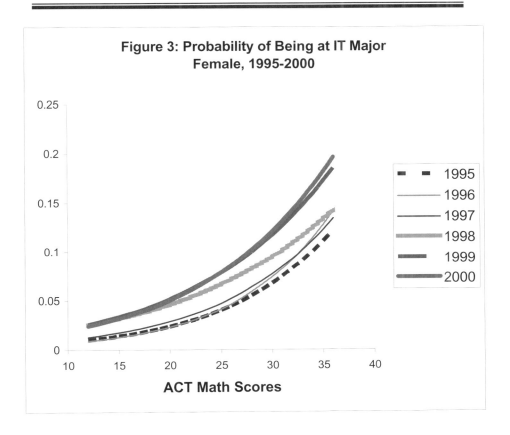

Figure 3: Probability of Being at IT Major Female, 1995-2000

It shows the impact on IT participation for women has increased significantly since 1995, with a slightly larger increase among those with high ACT scores. That is, women with stronger math ACT scores are increasingly more likely to become IT majors. A further analysis of the data though, shows that the gender gap has not narrowed. The differences in the two solid lines in Figure 4 represent the gender gap in math performance impact in 2000 while the two dashed lines represent the gender gap in 1995.

Hence the impact of math performance on IT participations has increased to a similar extent for both men and women from 1995 to 2000, leaving the gender gap persistent during this period.

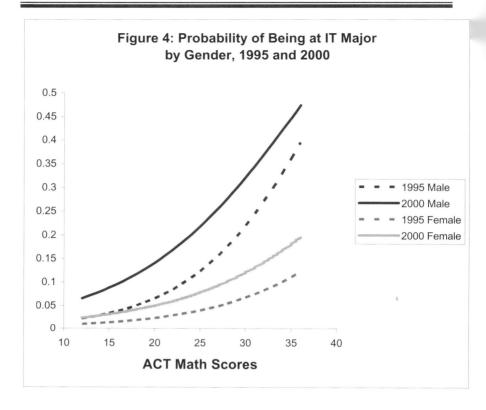

Figure 4: Probability of Being at IT Major by Gender, 1995 and 2000

ACT Math Scores

- - - 1995 Male
—— 2000 Male
- - - 1995 Female
—— 2000 Female

Conclusion

Since our society continues to value and reward IT professionals, any gender gap in high-IT core workforce will lead to greater gender income inequalities. It would also hinder economic growth since women constitute more than half of our labor force. Using student data from UIC we have documented the existence and persistence of a gender gap in IT majors. Since IT graduates are the primary source of the high-IT core workforce, the gender gap in IT majors will eventually translate into a gender gap in the high-IT core workforce. Our results show that the gender gap is a not a reflection of differences among ethnic groups. It exists within each of the ethnic groups. In addition, it is most significant for white students. Furthermore, while the gap has diminished over the last few years, it remained significant in 2000. Female IT majors would have to more than triple in 2000 in order to eliminate the gender gap. Moreover, while math performance is a significant predictor for becoming an IT major, it is less important for female students.

The results of our study, therefore, support the notion that while math performance is a dominant factor determining IT majors, differences in male-female math performance do not fully account for the technology gender gap. There are fewer girls of the same ability level as boys who take computer courses. Negative experience of girls in computer science classes where they often find themselves as one of the few female students evidently contributes to the technology gender gap. Parental and societal expectation that girls should not participate in science and technology also contribute to the gender gap. Girls' perception that computer s are "geeky," "lame ," or "boy stuff" would be another contributing factor. Lack of role models has also been cited as a cause for the lack of female participation in the technology area.

A change in societal and parental expectations regarding women's involvement in technology and correcting the male-only image of computer scientists will diminish the technology gender gap. Meanwhile, we should continue to encourage girls to build their math skills and stimulate their interest in exploring the use of technology to create new information and invent new ways to improve our lives.

References

Cooke, Sandra. 2000. "The Information Technology Workforce." *Digital Economy 2000*, Chapter V, U.S. Department of Commerce, June, http://www.esa.doc.gov/de2000.pdf.

Craver, Doris L. 1999. "Research Foundations for Improving the representation of Women in the Information Technology Workforce," Executive Summary, Virtual Workshop, held September 27 November 5, Directorate for Computer and Information Science and Engineering, National Science Foundation Report, http://www.nsf.gov/search97-cgi/vtopic .

Weinman Janice and Lisa Cain. 1999. "Technology - the New Gender Gap". *Technos*, Vol. 8, No. 1, Spring.

Notes

*Tam's research was partially funded by NSF award REC-0074604. We thank Joe Persky for his suggestions.

[1]A more technical version of this paper is forthcoming in *Removing Barriers: Women in Academic Science Technology Engineering and Mathematics*, (edited by Jill M. Bystyzienski and Sharon R.Bird).

Chapter 12

Race, the Digital Divide, and Workforce Readiness in Illinois

Cedric Herring

Technological innovation is essential to a dynamic, expanding economy. For employment and wage growth to occur, the economy must generate and adopt technological changes. The new economy of the digital age demands increased investments in education and training in the new technologies that keeps pace with such rapid change. But the supply of workers skilled in the emerging technologies has not kept pace with demand. Thus, despite the fact that there is no shortage of workers in the U.S., employers often lament the "skills shortage." Unfortunately, the skills gap has racial and ethnic dimensions that are tied to differential access to technology that has implications for workforce readiness.

In this chapter, I show that when we look at the racial and ethnic dimensions of this skills shortage and combine them with demographic trends, we see that the skills gap in the U.S. and in Illinois will probably become even wider. Both the nation and the state of Illinois are losing jobs in sectors that have the greatest percentage of racial and ethnic minorities at the same time that they are gaining jobs in sectors that have the smallest proportions of African Americans and Latinos. I point out that as a nation, we continue to train racial minorities for occupations with decreasing labor demands at the same time that we do not sufficiently prepare them for jobs that are opening up in sectors that lack skilled workers. This pattern leads to unemployment (i.e., a labor surplus) at the same time there is a shortage of skilled workers. This fact is punctuated by the additional observation that our greatest demographic growth is among those who are being least

165

prepared for jobs that are becoming available. After showing that the digital divide is reinforced in schools, at home, and in the workplace, I discuss the implications of these trends for remaining competitive in the new digital economy. Finally, I briefly discuss some proposals that can help bridge the digital divide that occurs along racial and ethnic lines.

Changing Computer Skills Requirements in America

Technology has had a major impact on what is required of workers. On-the-job computer use is growing in all jobs. According to data from the Current Population Surveys, the percentage of all individuals age 18 and over that reported using a computer at work grew between 1984 and 2003. As Figure 1 shows, in 1984, 25% of adults reported using a computer on the job. By 2003, this proportion had more than doubled and was up to 57%. Computer use at work is related to race and ethnicity. Figure 1 shows that the gap between blacks and whites grew from 7 percentage points in 1984 to 11 percentage points in 2003. Similarly, the gap between Hispanics and whites grew from 9 percentage points in 1984 to 16 percentage points in

Figure 1: Changes in the Percentage of Adults Who Use Computers at Work, 1984-2003

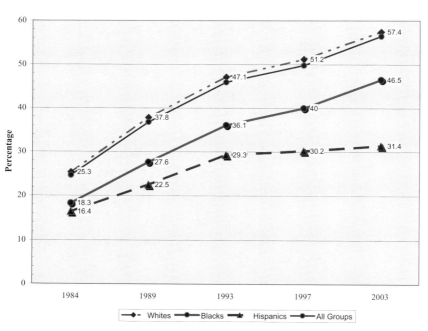

2003. On-the-job computer use is associated with one's occupation, as those in professional and managerial positions are the most likely to use computers as part of their work, and those in service jobs and positions as laborers are the least likely to use computers on the job. Nevertheless, there has been a general growth in computer use in all lines of work. Surveys of American businesses suggest that more than half of employers reported that restructuring and the introduction of new technology have increased the skill requirements even for non-managerial employees.

New growth areas usually arise from the development of new technologies. The expanding integration of Internet technologies by businesses, for example, has resulted in a rising demand for a variety of skilled workers who can develop and support Internet, Intranet, and web applications. The growth of electronic commerce means more establishments use the Internet to conduct their business online. This translates into a need for information technology professionals who can help firms use technology to communicate with employees, clients, and consumers. Explosive growth in these areas is also expected to fuel demand for specialists knowledgeable about network, data, and communications security. Indeed, the Bureau of Labor Statistics predicts that occupations such as "network systems and data communications analysts," and "computer software engineers," will be among the fastest growing jobs between 2002 and 2012 (Bureau of Labor Statistics, 2004). As a consequence, computer training, both formal and informal, was the most commonly received type of job-skills training. Thirty-eight percent of employees received formal computer training and 54% received informal training in computers while working for their current employers.

Employment of computing professionals is expected to increase much faster than average as technology becomes more sophisticated and organizations continue to adopt and integrate these technologies. Growth will be driven by very rapid growth in computer and data processing services, and software publishing is projected to be the fastest growing industry in the U.S. economy (Bureau of Labor Statistics, 2004).

The growing demand for skill is evident in the premium employers are willing to pay for workers with education and computer training. In 2004, the median annual earnings of computer systems analysts were $100,110, and the median annual earnings of computer software engineers were $83,460. Salaries for computer-related occupations ranged from $50,000 to $73,800 for security administrators, $51,500 to $73,000 for webmasters, and from $47,000 to $65,500 for web developers.

Figure 2 shows that African Americans and Hispanics are under-represented in the fastest growing, high skill occupational types that pay well. For example, 22% of blacks and 15% of Hispanics hold professional and managerial occupations. This compares with 32% of whites. In contrast, 22% of blacks and 20% of Hispanics hold service-oriented occupations compared with 12% of whites. And 18% of blacks and 22% of Hispanics have jobs as machine and equipment operators and laborers compared with 12% of whites. African Americans comprise 14% of the U.S. population and 9% of the workforce, but they make up 6.6% of computer-related occupations. Similarly, Hispanics are 16% of the U.S. population and 10% of the workforce, but they constitute 4% of those working in computer-

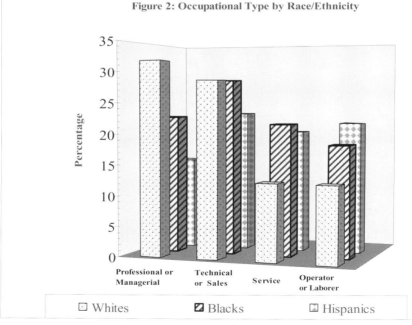

Figure 2: Occupational Type by Race/Ethnicity

related occupations. Clearly, race and ethnicity are related to kinds of jobs people perform, and this is clearly the case in rapidly expanding and high paying computer-related fields. When access to jobs is associated with access to technology, those who have better access to technology will also have advantages in securing jobs. Those with little or no access to technology will be disadvantaged and marginalized. So common justice clearly demands that we should strive for equitable access and, in particular, to ensure that members of low-access communities are not further disadvantaged by exclusion from the digital world.

Race/Ethnicity and the Digital Divide

In the new digital economy, some people have the best information technology that the nation has to offer. These people have the most powerful computers, the best communications systems, the fastest Internet connections, and a wealth of content and training relevant to their lives. There is another group of people who, for various reasons, do not have access to computers or Internet services. The difference between these two groups of people is part of the digital divide.

To be on the less fortunate side of the divide means that there is less opportunity to take part in the new information-based economy, in which many more jobs will be related to computers. It also means that there is less opportunity to take part in the education, training, shopping, entertainment and communications opportunities that are available online. Now that a large number of Americans regularly use the Internet to conduct daily activities, people who lack access to those tools are at a growing disadvantage. Therefore, raising the level of digital inclusion by increasing the number of Americans using the technology tools of the digital age is an important goal.

The digital divide in computer ownership between white and African American households grew between 1984 and 2003. As Figure 3 shows, the white-black gap in computer ownership went from a 5 percentage point difference to more than a 21 percentage point difference. For white versus Hispanic households, the gap similarly rose from a 4.5 point gap to a 22 percentage point gap. Minorities are also losing ground with regard to

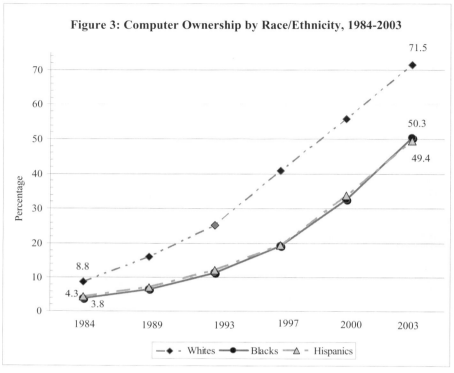

Figure 3: Computer Ownership by Race/Ethnicity, 1984-2003

Internet access. Between 1997 and 2003, the gap between white and black households increased from a 13.5 percentage point difference to a 22.6 percentage point difference. The white-Hispanic gap went from a 12.5 percentage point difference to a 22.5 percentage point difference. In short, there is still a yawning divide among different races and ethnic groups.

What does the future hold? A well-known truism is "the children are our future." But if they are, there are reasons to be less than optimistic. For example, among the youth (as well as among adults), there is a racial technology gap that has major implications for educational attainment and workplace readiness in the future.

A 1995 Department of Education report indicated that, nationwide, black and Hispanic children were 30% less likely than white children to have Internet access computers in their classrooms. Even when computers were available in schools, the ratio of students to computers was nearly twice as

Figure 4: Percentage of Children with Computers and Internet Access at Home by Race/Ethnicity

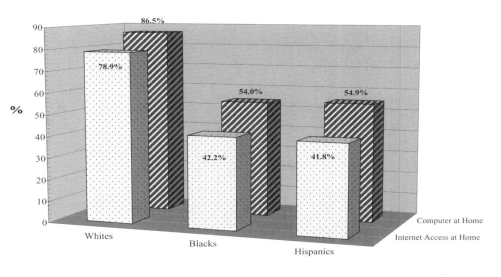

high in inner-city schools as in the suburbs. Data from the October 2003 Current Population Survey suggest that there are still large racial disparities. As Figure 4 shows, there is a 31.5 percentage point difference between white and black students in computer access at home. The difference between whites and Hispanics is just about as large, at a 30.9 percentage point difference. Figure 4 also presents data on Internet access and usage. This chart shows that the racial digital divide is even larger on this dimension. Less than half of African American children (42.2%) and Hispanic children (41.8%) have access to the Internet at home. In contrast, nearly 8 in 10 (78.9%) of white children have Internet access at home.

If computer literacy in the future will be as necessary as basic literacy is now, both at home and at school, these patterns suggest that blacks and Hispanics are more likely to be at the periphery of the computer and e-commerce revolution in the 21st century. While some people will be able to speed down the information superhighway with faster and faster connections to the Internet, others will be relegated to the back streets of technological illiteracy. Such a technology gap will reinforce great social and economic disparities, as computer skills are likely to be prerequisites for the workplace of the 21st century.

Patterns in Illinois

What about in Illinois? It has been projected that the Illinois economy will require nearly 7 million workers by the year 2008. Each year over 80,000 job openings on average will need to be filled. Professional and technical occupations and service occupations will add the most new jobs through 2008. These two groups cover a wide range of occupations, including: engineers, financial managers, pre-school and kindergarten teachers, occupational therapy assistants, information technology occu-pations, human services workers, medical assistants, corrections officers, etc. If these new jobs are to be filled by skilled workers who are prepared for the demands of these positions, it will require a reversal of some basic patterns that are currently taking place.

As mentioned in the first chapter of this volume, population changes have not been evenly distributed in Illinois. The number of non-Hispanic whites decreased from 8.5 million in 1990 to 8.4 million by 2003. This represented a decrease of about 1.6%. In contrast, the number of Hispanic (non-black) residents increased from about 850,000 in 1990 to more than 1.7 million in 2003–an increase of more than 100%. The number of blacks in Illinois increased from 1.7 million in 1990 to 1.9 million in 2003. This represented an increase of 13%. The number of Asians and others also increased from just over 300,000 in 1990 to over 600,000 in 2003. This represents a 98% increase.

People of color constitute a third (33%) of the population of Illinois. The number of African Americans and Hispanics in Illinois will continue to grow, while it is projected that the white population will continue to decline. These demographic trends should portend greater numbers of African American and Hispanic workers. Yet, blacks and Hispanics are the racial and ethnic groups that have the least (racially and ethnically) proportional representation in the upper echelons of the workforce. As mentioned previously, there is a racial technology gap that has major implications for educational attainment and workplace readiness in the future.

Job growth in the new economy is inextricably linked to changes in technology. In particular, the revolution in computers and telecommunications is creating unprecedented changes. It is bringing about new jobs, an explosion in entrepreneurship and trade, access to education and new forms of information, and new modes of community building. All of these things and many more are dividends of this revolution in information technology. Yet, the fruits of the new digital economy are out of reach for many. The digital divide threatens to cut off populations from good jobs and the chance to participate in the affairs of the broader society. For some citizens technology brings the promise of inclusion, opportunity, and wealth; for others, the lack of access to such resources means greater isolation and increased poverty.

Figure 5 presents the percentage of Illinois adults who have computers at home and the percentage who have access to the Internet at home. These results parallel what we have seen before: there is a substantial

Figure 5: Percentage of Illinois Adults with Computers and Internet Access at Home by Race/Ethnicity

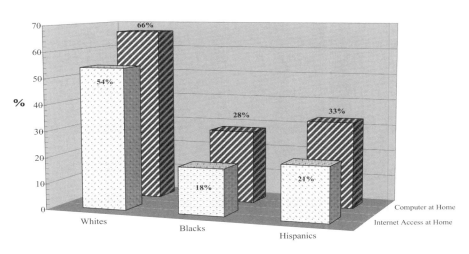

□ Internet Access at Home   ☑ Computer at Home

173

digital divide between whites, on the one hand, and blacks and Hispanics on the other. In particular, according to data from the 2003 Current Population Survey, 28% of blacks and 33% of Hispanics in Illinois have computers at home. This compares with 66% of whites who have computers at home. Similarly, 18% of blacks and 21% of Hispanics have access to the Internet at home compared with 54% of whites.

These numbers reveal that the digital divide in Illinois not only still exists, but is wider than the gap on the national level. The gap in computer ownership between white and black households continues to grow, as does the gap between white and Hispanic households. Blacks and Hispanics are losing ground even faster with regard to Internet access. Despite the growing use of online services, communities in nearly one-quarter of Illinois zip codes do not have access to high-speed Internet service.

What Can Be Done to Close the Digital Divide?

The Digital Divide Elimination Infrastructure Fund was established as part of Illinois' telecommunications reform package passed in 2001. It was intended to subsidize the construction of high-speed Internet service or advanced telecommunications infrastructure in rural areas of the state. However, the original eligibility requirements were too restrictive–only companies that had been waived of the responsibility for providing advanced telecommunications services could apply. As a result, no grants were released.

In 2005, HB2478 was introduced to amend the Digital Divide Elimination Act of 2001. The proposed legislation would create the Non-profit Digital Divide Foundation to make grants for the establishment and expansion of Community Technology Centers and for assisting public hospitals, libraries, and park districts in eliminating the digital divide. It also allows the Foundation to accept and solicit funds from a variety of sources. Community technology centers would be used to provide computer and technology access to individuals, communities, and populations that typically would not otherwise have places to use computer and telecommunications technologies.

This legislation is an additional step in the right direction that will help close the digital divide that exists along racial lines. Even bolder steps, however, would include municipal or community-based wireless (i.e., Wi-Fi) networks. Philadelphia, for example, recently became the first major city in the nation to offer city-wide high-speed wireless Internet service. Access costs $20 per month, and low-income residents are eligible to pay half that amount. In effect, the new Wi-Fi service can be viewed as just another city utility, as city property can be used to locate necessary transmitters and equipment. This "Wi-Fi-as-utility policy" is not a policy that could only be implemented in cities. Several smaller towns and suburban areas have been offering their residents such services for years. If the State of Illinois were to promote such bold steps in Illinois counties and municipalities, it could take giant steps in eliminating the digital divide, making the state more competitive technologically, reducing its costs in delivering services to state residents, generating additional revenue for the state's coffers, preparing current and future workers for jobs in the 21st century, and still saving a great deal of money for Illinois taxpayers who currently pay substantially more for Internet access.

Conclusions

The data reveal a number of trends. On the positive side, it is apparent that all Americans are becoming increasingly connected by computer and the Internet over time. On the other hand, it is also apparent that access for certain groups is growing far more rapidly, particularly with respect to Internet connectivity. This pattern means that the "haves" are becoming more information-rich while the "have nots" are falling even further behind.

As the Internet becomes a more mature and pervasive technology, the digital divide among households of different races, incomes, and education levels may narrow. Even so, it is reasonable to expect that many people are going to lag behind for a long time unless there is some type of intervention. This has profound implications for the workforce. For example, although the 7.2% unemployment rate for blacks in September of 2000 was the lowest ever recorded, it was still more than double the rate for whites (3.5%). Moreover, African Americans continued to be underrepresented in managerial and professional jobs, as well as in the jobs projected to grow the fastest into the next century: those that require the development or use of information technology.

Education and income appear to be among the leading elements driving the racial digital divide today. Relative to white workers, fewer African Americans and Hispanics have college degrees, and even fewer have degrees in math, science, or engineering. African Americans and Hispanics, on average, tend to score lower on tests of reading and mathematics proficiency than whites. But even beyond this basic skills gap, there appears to be racial differences in access to computers and emerging technologies that have work-relevant consequences. These realities merit thoughtful responses by policymakers consistent with the needs of Americans in the digital age.

This chapter has tried to show that when we look at the racial and ethnic dimensions of the skills shortage and combine them with demographic trends, we see that the skills gap in the U.S. and in Illinois will probably become even wider. It showed that in Illinois, we are gaining jobs in sectors where the growing segments of the population–blacks and Hispanics–are proportionately underrepresented. The growing digital divide will exacerbate the racial gap in preparedness for high-paying, skilled jobs that are becoming available. To fill these jobs and remain competitive in the 21st century, the residents of Illinois will need additional skills and job training. Government, business, and community institutions can all play a role in ensuring that this happens. Specifically, legislation that promotes municipal or community-based wireless (i.e., Wi-Fi) networks would help decrease the digital divide and make the state more competitive technologically while potentially reducing costs to state residents.

References

Bureau of Labor Statistics. 2004. BLS Releases 2002-12 *Employment Projections*. Washington: United States Department of Labor.

Bureau of Labor Statistics. 2003. *October 2003 Current Population Survey (CPS) CPS Supplement Files*. Machine-Readable Electronic Data File.

About the Contributors

Editor

Cedric Herring (PhD, University of Michigan) is Professor in the Department of Sociology at the University of Illinois at Chicago and in the Institute of Government and Public Affairs at the University of Illinois. Dr. Herring is former President of the Association of Black Sociologists, and he was the Founding Director of the Institute for Research on Race and Public Policy at UIC. He has published widely on topics such as social policy (e.g., social welfare and affirmative action), labor force issues and policy, stratification and inequality, and the sociology of African Americans. He has published four books and more than 50 scholarly articles. His books include *African Americans and the Public Agenda: The Paradoxes of Publi c Policy,* and most recently, *Skin Deep: How Race and Complexion Matter in the Color-Blind Era*. He has also received support for his research from the National Science Foundation, the Ford Foundation, the MacArthur Foundation, the Joyce Foundation, and others. Dr. Herring has shared his findings in community forums, in newspapers and magazines, on radio and television, before government officials, and at the United Nations.

Authors

Gilbert W. Bassett, Jr. is Professor and Head of the Department of Finance at the University of Illinois at Chicago. He is a long-term affiliate of the Institute of Government and Public Affairs in Chicago. His research interests include statistics; financial markets; energy and the environment, and diversity issues. Recent publications include Does Diversity Matter? Measuring the Impact of High School Diversity on Freshman GPA (with Mo-Yin S. Tam); New Selection Indices for University Admissions: A Quantile Approach (with Mo-Yin S. Tam and Uday Sukhatme); and Robust Voting (with Joseph Persky). He was the Alumni Research Award Winner at UIC in 1997 and the Alumni Teaching Award Winner in 1996. He received his PhD in Economics in 1973 from the University of Michigan.

Cinthia Elkins is an MD/PhD student in the Medical Scholars Program at the University of Illinois at Champaign-Urbana, and the Department of Community Health. She is a Research Assistant for Professor Robert F. Rich at the U of IL Institute of Government and Public Affairs. Her research interests include health policy, access to health care, health care disparities, and rural health policy.

Christopher T. Erb is an M.D. / Ph.D. candidate in the Medical Scholars Program and Department of Community Health at the University of Illinois at Urbana-Champaign. Mr. Erb is also a Ruth L. Kirschstein pre-doctoral fellow of the National Institute of Mental Health. His research interests include health care policy and law in the age of managed care, mental health policy and law, disability policy and law, and international comparative health care policy. His dissertation research focuses on state level mental health policy making in the era of managed care. Mr. Erb's work has been published in the *American Journal of Public Health*, the *DePaul Journal of Health Care Law*, the *Illinois Law Review*, the *Stanford Law and Policy Review*, and the *Elder Law Journal*. He is co-editor (with Robert F. Rich) of the book *Consumer Choice: Social Welfare and Health Policy*, published in 2005.

J. Fred Giertz is a Professor of economics and member of the Institute of Government and Public Affairs at the University of Illinois at Urbana-Champaign. He has held this position since 1980. He received his Ph. D. in economics from Northwestern University in Evanston, Illinois in 1970. Professor Giertz's major research interests are in the areas of public finance, public choice, and regional economic development. He specializes in state and local taxation and expenditure analysis and in regional economic development issues. He has consulted with a variety of different governments, firms, and other organizations on tax and economic development issues. Professor Giertz follows general macroeconomic issues, especially as they impact Illinois. He also writes frequently on Illinois budget issues in publications such as State Tax Notes and compiles the U of I Flash Index, a monthly indicator of the Illinois economy. He is also a columnist for *State Tax Notes*. Beginning in 1995, Professor Giertz served ten years a member of the board of trustees of the State Universities Retirement System (SURS) including a term as the chair of the board's investment committee. The board oversees the $12.5 billion retirement fund for Illinois public university and college employees. In 2000, he was named the Executive Director of the National Tax Association, a 1,600 member organization of tax professionals located in Washington, D. C.

Rachel Gordon is an Assistant Professor of sociology at the University of Illinois at Chicago and a faculty member of the Institute of Government and Public Affairs. Gordon's primary research areas include (1) welfare and employment policies, especially as they relate to early family formation, (2) measuring and modeling the contexts of families' lives, and (3) the application of longitudinal research methods to study of children and families. She has published a number of papers regarding the association between community context and child well being, the causes and consequences of grandmother co-residential support for young mothers, the relationships between youth gang participation and delinquency, and the evaluation of social programs. She currently directs two programs at IGPA: the Family Impact Seminars, a series of briefings for state legislators on family policy issues, and NEW Leadership Illinois, a week-long residential summer institute for college women designed to increase women's representation in all elements of public life, including elected office. She has received research funding from the National Science Foundation, the U.S. Department of Health and Human Services and the U.S. Department of Labor and funding for policy activities from the MacArthur Foundation and the Foundation for Child Development.

Lorens A. Helmchen, Ph.D., is an Assistant Professor in the Division of Health Policy and Administration at the School of Public Health, University of Illinois at Chicago. He holds a joint appointment at the University's Institute of Government and Public Affairs and a research appointment in the Department of Economics. Dr. Helmchen earned a Ph.D. in economics from the University of Chicago in 2004 and wrote his doctoral dissertation on the economics of rising obesity prevalence in the United States. He also holds an M.A. in economics from Humboldt University, Berlin, Germany, and spent a year at the Ecole Nationale de la Statistique et de l'Administration Economique, Paris, France. Dr. Helmchen's current research interests include the optimal design of provider reimbursement, organizational innovation in the hospital industry, the effect of pay-for-performance on the market for physicians, and the economics of nutrition and exercise. He teaches health economics and microeconometrics.

Madhu Khanna is a Professor in the Department of Agricultural and Consumer Economics at the University of Illinois at Urbana-Champaign. Her research analyzes the performance of alternative environmental policy instruments and environmentally friendly technologies for pollution control. She also examines the effectiveness of voluntary initiatives by corporations and land owners to improve environmental performance and the targeting of green payment policies for preventing nonpoint pollution from crop production.

Peter F. Mulhall, Ph.D. is the Director of Center for Prevention Research and Development Institute of Government and Public Affairs and an adjunct faculty member in the Department of Community Health at the University of Illinois Urbana-Champaign. Dr. Mulhall has over 20 years many years experience in community health education and prevention with a special emphasis on adolescent problem behaviors (school failure, teen pregnancy, substance abuse, violence, and organizations that serve them. Most recently, he has worked with several state and federal agencies developing and reporting performance measures for assessing capacity, process and outcomes for prevention and early intervention programs for youth. He also served on the method groups for the development of the Performance Partnership Initiative and Core Measures Initiative with the Substance Abuse and Mental Health Services Administration (SAMSHA) and the Carter Center Forum on Performance Measures. Dr. Mulhall is currently a member of the Illinois Advisory Board for Collaborative for Academic, Social, Emotional Learning (CASEL), Illinois Children's Mental Health Partnership Evaluation Advisory Committee, and the Leadership Team for the Illinois, Afterschool Partnership. Dr. Mulhall has published and presented numerous papers on adolescent health issues, preventive interventions, evaluation methods, and performance management. Dr. Mulhall and the staff at CPRD are currently have funding from Illinois Department of Human Services, U.S. Department of Education, Kraft Corporation, U.S. Center for Substance Abuse Prevention, and several other local and national organizations.

Naoko Muramatsu is an Associate Professor in the Division of Community Health Sciences, School of Public Health, the University of Illinois at Chicago and a Visiting faculty member of the University of Illinois Institute of Government and Public Affairs. She is also a visiting researcher at the National Institute of Public Health in Japan. Her research interests include long-term care policies, access to and quality of health services, health and well being of older adults, long-term care workforce, and cross-cultural studies of aging and health. She is currently Principal Investigator of an NIA-funded study on State Long-term Care Policies and Elderly Well Being. Her research articles have appeared in the Journal of Gerontology: Social Sciences, The Gerontologist, Journal of Health and Social Behavior, Journal of the American Geriatrics Society, and Health Services Research. Dr. Muramatsu obtained a PhD in Health Services Organization and Policy in 1995 as well as Master's degrees in Sociology and Health Services Administration respectively in 1995 and 1993, all from the University of Michigan. Dr. Muramatsu has received a number of awards, including a Fulbright Scholarship.

Elizabeth Powers is an Associate Professor in the Department of Economics and in the Institute of Government and Public Affairs at the University of Illinois in Urbana-Champaign. Professor Powers' current research is concentrated on proposed Social Security reform and its potential impact on Social Security programs other than retirement benefits. Additionally, Professor Powers is interested in child health, with her study on "Child Disability and Maternal Labor Force Participation" having received the Arnold O. Beckman Award, given by the UIUC Research Board for projects of special distinction, special promise, or special resource value. Professor Powers has been at the University of Illinois since August 1996. Prior to coming to Illinois, she served for three years as an economist with the Federal Reserve Bank of Cleveland. From 1989 to 1990 she was a junior staff economist with President Bush's Council of Economic Advisers. Professor Powers organized a conference on child well-being for IGPA, as well as a major conference on child care policy. She also recently made a presentation on "A New Funding Regime for Welfare" to the Illinois Congressional Delegation. Professor Powers holds a PhD in economics from the University of Pennsylvania.

Kent Redfield is a Professor of Political Studies at the University of Illinois-Springfield (UIS). He is currently serving as the interim director for the Institute for Legislative Studies, when he has been a research fellow since 1979. Dr. Redfield has an appointment in the Institute of Government and Public Affairs. In addition, He is also the Director of the Sunshine Project, a campaign finance research project funded by the Joyce Foundation. He received his undergraduate degree in political science from the University of Utah and his M.A. and Ph.D. in political science from the University of Washington. Prior to joining the faculty at the University of Illinois - Springfield in 1979, Dr. Redfield worked for four years as a member of the research/appropriations staff for the Speaker of the Illinois General Assembly. Dr. Redfield directed the Illinois Legislative Staff Intern Program for 20 years before stepping down from the program in 1999. In his current position, he supervises the director of the intern program. He is a co-author of *Lawmaking in Illinois* and a contributor to the *Almanac of Illinois Politics,* which is now in its sixth edition. Dr. Redfield has been engaged in research on the financing of political campaigns in Illinois and political ethics since 1991. The results of that research have been presented in numerous research reports, a series of articles in *Illinois Issues*, a 1994 book on financing legislative elections in Illinois, which is entitled *Cash Clout* and a 2001 book on the role of money in Illinois politics entitled *Money Counts*.

Robert F. Rich is Director of in the Institute of Government and Public Affairs. In addition, he is Professor in IGPA, the College of Medicine, the Political Science Department and the College of Law. His research focuses on health law and policy, federalism and the role of the states, environmental policy, and science policy. He has published five books and forty articles. He has also served as a consultant for a wide variety of federal and state government agencies. Professor Rich is the founder and former director of the Office of Pubic Management of IGPA, which offers educational programs to elected and non-elected local government officials. In addition, he serves as the coordinator for the local and state government strategic initiative of the Partnership Illinois Program. Robert Rich was named a Faculty Fellow in the Office of the Vice Chancellor for Public Engagement and Institutional Relations for the 2003-04, 04-05, 05-06 academic years. Dr. Rich has also been named a Permanent Fellow in the European Center for the Comparative Government and Public Policy, a .center funded by the Humboldt University, the Technical University, and the Free University of Berlin. In addition to his appointed positions, he has been elected as the Vice president of the Board of the Warren and Clara Cole Foundation; a health care research foundation in Chicago. Finally, Dr. Rich was invited by the U.S. State Department for a lecture tour in (Frankfurt, Munich, Stuttgart, Nurenberg, and Berlin) Germany where he lectured on health law and policy, federalism, and the future of the social contract.

Mo-Yin Tam is Professor of Economics and Associate Vice Chancellor for Academic Affairs at the University of Illinois at Chicago. Her research interests include diversity; the economics of education; the digital divide; incentive schemes and Pareto optimality; and income distributions and welfare implications. She was the recipient of a National Science Foundation award for "POWRE, Digital Divide, IT Workforce and High School Quality" from the Division of Research, Evaluation and Communication, Directorate for Education and Human Resources. She received her PhD in Economics in 1974 from the State University of New York at Stony Brook.

182